SIMPLY
SALMON

Published in 2001 by
Stewart, Tabori & Chang
A division of Harry N. Abrams, Inc.
115 West 18th Street
New York, NY 10011

Library of Congress Cataloguing-in-Publication Data
Peterson, James.
Simply salmon/James Peterson.
p. cm.
Includes index.
ISBN 1-58479-026-1
1. Cookery (Salmon) 2. Salmon. 1. Title.

TX748.S24 P48 2001
641.6'92—dc21
00-067888

Printed in Singapore

109876543

DESIGN BY NINA BARNETT

SIMPLY
SALMON

James Peterson

STEWART, TABORI & CHANG

NEW YORK

CONTENTS

INTRODUCTION

During the early 1980s, I owned a small French restaurant in Manhattan. In those days, it wasn't so easy to find the luxurious foods we encounter today, and certain fish were especially hard to find and exorbitantly expensive. As hard as it is to imagine now, salmon was such a fish—it was virtually all wild, caught in Alaska or the West Coast, and little of it made it to the East Coast. My urban fish hunting was made no easier by the business hours at the Fulton Fish Market where wholesale fish were sold—from 3 to 7 A.M. Since I had to get up early to get to the restaurant and staying up to 3 A.M. to hit the fish market wasn't an option, I had the brilliant idea of calling a wholesale fish dealer and have him pick me out a salmon and save it so I could come by and pick it up later in the day. (Since I shopped by taxi—a system that helped lead to the restaurant's eventual demise—my typical day started out with an irate cab driver yelling about my fish smelling up his cab or the freshly killed ducks leaking blood on the floor.) When I arrived at the fish store—it didn't occur to me to have it delivered—I beheld my salmon: it was covered with a thick layer of white slime (the fish guy tried to convince me this was a sign of freshness), its eyes looked in need of serious cataract surgery, and its aroma was, well, fishy. Very fishy.

Shortly after my salmon trauma an importer suggested I try some salmon that was being farm-raised in Norway. I was skeptical—farm-raised fish was still very unusual—but decided to give it a try. The creature cost a small fortune since it was air freighted packed in ice and was still a relatively rare commodity. But when I opened the Styrofoam box I saw a beautiful fish, bright silver with black clear eyes, still slippery from the sea, and smelling like an immaculate beach. From then on salmon became a part of our regular menu

Whole Salmon Baked in Salt (see page 129).

and remained a rather special and luxurious dish until all the other chefs in New York started buying and serving the same salmon from Norway.

Now salmon is farmed all over the world, competition has brought prices down and quality up. Wild salmon from the West Coast appears in much better condition when it's in season, which traditionally has been from late spring through early fall, but now for some species is year round. While not exactly cheap, salmon is less expensive and of consistently better quality that most other fish you're likely to encounter at the fish market. Salmon is also easy to cook because it has a full flavor (making it perfect for grilling), a firm texture that makes it easy to handle, and a fairly high fat content (miraculously, experts say salmon fat is good for you) that keeps it from drying out if you overcook it a little.

But why a book about salmon, especially when I've already written a long, comprehensive book called *Fish & Shellfish*? Because for many of us salmon is the only fish we ever cook. After the publication of *Fish & Shellfish*, I asked a lot of people why they'll only eat fish in a restaurant and rarely if ever at home. Well, it turns out that for most people, buying fish is like buying a used car. They're sure they're being sold some ancient thing, and half the time they are. But because salmon is distributed very efficiently, and precisely because it has become so popular that it turns over quickly in stores, we can be reasonably sure that what we buy is fresh. Salmon is also available in convenient sizes—fillets or steaks—and, especially when sold as fillets, is easily made boneless. Salmon also has idiosyncrasies that allow you to cook it in ways that wouldn't work for other fish. When grilled or sautéed its skin is delicious—although some people have the same aversion to fish skin as they do to fish heads—and it can be cooked using practically any method.

Simply Salmon is organized according to cooking technique and includes virtually every method used for cooking fish (I left out steaming because I think it's a bore) so that once you make one or two of the (for the most part) simple recipes, you'll master the technique and be able to invent variations of your own. When I teach cooking I always try to get students to cook using a basic technique and their own common sense and intuition about what ingredients go best with what. When I cook a dish, I never cook it exactly the same way twice. Some little method or ingredient suggests itself somewhere in the process, a source of constant frustration for my students who end up looking desperately back and forth between me and their recipes.

So I hope this little book will arm you with the recipes and techniques you need to prepare what may very well be your favorite fish.

Ivory Salmon en Papillote (see page 126).

THE BASICS

Though most of us know a salmon when we see one, not all salmon are the same. In East Coast stores we're most likely to encounter farm-raised Atlantic salmon and, less frequently, Pacific salmon, while on the West Coast, the reverse is true. There are a number of species of Pacific salmon—many of which are wild, some of which are farmed—but only one species of Atlantic salmon, practically all of which is farmed. Farmed Atlantic salmon is sold already gutted and in fairly standardized sizes, usually 8 to 12 pounds, 40 percent of which are bones and head. Even though Pacific and Atlantic salmon look similar, they are not only different species, but also members of different genera. Both Pacific and Atlantic salmon are, however, members of the same family *Salmonidae*, which includes trout and Arctic char.

While farmed Atlantic salmon is all pretty much the same, Pacific salmon is made up of several species and may be caught at different stages in the salmon's life cycle, all of which affect the taste and texture of what ends up on your plate. Salmon live both in fresh water, where they hatch, and in salt water, where they grow up, swim around, and eat before working their way back up the same river where they hatched to spawn. Wild salmon are often sold by the name of their favorite river. This is why you sometime see "Columbia River salmon" from Washington or Oregon, "Copper River salmon" from Alaska, and even "Sacramento River salmon" from California.

There are seven species of Pacific salmon: chinook (usually called king salmon, and occasionally spring salmon), sockeye, coho, chum, pink, Japanese cherry (*masu*, found only in Japan), and steelhead, which has recently been

A whole Atlantic salmon with one fillet removed.

reclassified as salmon and is often referred to as "steelhead salmon." Because chinook (king) salmon is considered the best and is priced accordingly, it's worthwhile knowing how to recognize one. King salmon have black spots running along their back and more importantly black spots on their tail, but the real giveaway are their black gums. Wild king salmon is harvested year round but its peak season is March to October. Farmed king salmon and farmed coho salmon are available year round. Copper River salmon, perhaps the most prized, is available in the late spring. A small percentage of king salmon have pale, almost white flesh and are now being marketed under the name "ivory salmon." Ivory salmon have become fashionable, partly because they have a particular delicate flavor all their own. If you're buying Pacific salmon in the winter it's probably been frozen, not an entirely bad thing especially if you're eating it raw or curing or smoking it (see Serving Raw Salmon, page 117). Chinook salmon (usually called king salmon) can be very large (up to 100 pounds) but most wild kings you see at the fish store weigh between 15 and 20 pounds. Farmed king salmon are generally smaller, from 5 to 15 pounds.

Sockeye salmon (also sometimes called blueback or red salmon) have the reddest flesh of all salmon. Sockeye is popular on the West Coast because of its red flesh, high oil content (which gives it flavor), and convenient size—anywhere from 2 to 8 pounds. Since the Japanese are particularly fond of it, you're likely to see it at high quality sushi bars. Sockeye salmon are considered to be comparable in quality to chinook salmon. You're unlikely to see a whole sockeye salmon at the fish market, but if you do, it's likely to be expensive. From the outside sockeye salmon look like chum salmon, which are of lower quality and should be cheaper. When looking at whole fish, telling the difference isn't always easy unless you see the two side by side, but sockeyes usually have smaller eyes. Once filleted or cut into steaks, sockeye salmon is easy to recognize by its deep red flesh.

Wild coho salmon (also called silver salmon) are caught from Oregon to Alaska, with the peak season during July and August. Wild coho salmon usually weigh between 5 and 12 pounds but coho salmon are also farmed and sold at about 1 pound, the weight of a good-sized trout. Coho salmon flesh is usually deep red and slightly more orange than sockeye. Again, telling the difference between a coho salmon and some other kind of salmon takes some experience. Unlike king salmon, which have tails completely covered with black spots, coho salmon only have spots at the top of the tail and are lightly spotted all along the top, from tail to head. Unlike king salmon, which have black gums, a coho salmon's lower gum is white. The end of a coho's tail is relatively flat compared to the less expensive chum salmon, which has a more distinctly V-shaped tail and hardly any spots.

Chum salmon is one of the most abundant Pacific salmon, especially in the late summer and early fall. It generally weighs from 8 to 15 pounds and varies in quality depending on what stage in its life cycle it was caught. While chum salmon is perfectly good, it's flesh isn't as firm or rich as that from other salmon, and because you shouldn't be buying chum salmon at king salmon prices, it helps to recognize one. Chum salmon have fewer spots than other species of salmon and those they do have are scattered here and there without much regularity. The tail is distinctly V-shaped. Since the quality of chum salmon varies considerably, it's graded according to the amount of dark coloring—called water marks—on its skin. There are three distinct categories: silver-brite (bright silver and considered the best, occasionally called keta salmon), semi-brites, which are slightly darker and have paler flesh, and darks, which have the darkest skin and the palest flesh. Once chum salmon has been cut into fillets or steaks, it's best to judge its quality by its color—the darker red, the better (unlike king salmon, which is often tastier when paler).

Pink salmon are the smallest salmon and spoil more quickly than larger species. Because of this they have traditionally been used for canning, but I often spot them in ethnic markets where they are inexpensive and a perfect size—about 3 to 5 pounds—for grilling or roasting whole. Pink salmon are easy to spot because the other species are rarely marketed at such a small size. Pink salmon are also more gray and less silvery than other species and have black oval spots covering their tails. The best pink salmon have the firmest flesh—your finger won't leave an imprint—and are a bargain. As the name implies, pink salmon have pink rather than red flesh.

Wild Versus Farmed: Because wild Atlantic salmon never appears for sale and is only caught by sports fisherman, few of us have the opportunity to compare wild and farmed Atlantic salmon. Any wild salmon we encounter at the fish market is Pacific salmon, which is leaner than Atlantic salmon and whose taste varies widely depending on where and when it was caught. Most everyone says that wild salmon is better than farmed salmon, but I remain unconvinced. Farmed salmon is consistently flavorful and since it is shipped out as soon as it is killed and gutted, it is almost always impeccably fresh. Farmed salmon is also less red than most wild salmon, although it can be made redder with special feed—redness has little to do with quality. Despite being content with the quality of farmed salmon, I still eat wild salmon when it's in season and I can find it (it also, at least on the East Coast, is a lot more expensive) simply because it's different, not because it's necessarily better. True, I occasionally happen upon a fish that has a celestial flavor but every fish is slightly different, an element of unpredictability that makes eating wild salmon more interesting.

Farmed Salmon: Some Ifs, Ands, or Buts: While farmed salmon has provided us with a plentiful source of fresh, beautiful salmon, modern salmon farming techniques often have a negative environmental impact. Salmon that is farmed in open pens—the most common method used today—release a number of contaminants into the surrounding water and can do damage to the surrounding eco-system. As home cooks and restaurant chefs become more aware of this problem, we can insist on more environmentally friendly salmon farming methods. One such method uses a closed pen with its own attached water treatment system. Another method consists of acclimatizing young salmon to salt water in open pens but then releasing them where they can grow to maturity in the wild and where they can be bought using traditional farming methods. It is also possible to avoid farmed salmon altogether and buy only wild Pacific salmon, some of which is in season for more than half the year. When fresh wild salmon is not available, high quality "frozen at sea (FAS)" can be used during the off season.

Judging Freshness: Because nowadays most salmon available in the market is farmed and the systems for getting it from the farm to the plate are much more efficient than they were in the past, most salmon, at least when it arrives at the fish store, is in excellent condition. Salmon also keeps better than other fish, so a whole salmon that's several days old and has been properly stored will still be fresh.

Salmon is sold whole (always gutted), cut crosswise into steaks, or in fillets. It is no exception to the rule that it's easier to judge the freshness of whole fish than filleted fish or fish that's been cut into steaks. A whole salmon should be so shiny that it sparkles. The skin should be silvery with no dark or gray

A skin-on salmon fillet.

patches—where scales were rubbed off from mishandling—and the eyes crystal clear and protruding slightly from the head. Lift the cartilaginous flap at the base of the head (called the opercle) or have the fish seller do it so you can look at the gills. The gills should be deep red or pink, and when you stick your nose near them they should have a clean sea-like odor with nothing fishy about them. The end of the tail should be straight and moist and not curling up or drying out at the end.

Judging the freshness of fillets and steaks and making sure you're getting the freshest pieces may require a little subterfuge. First, buy your salmon in a store that looks and smells clean (again, no fishy smell) with the fish carefully arranged on ice in the display cases and fillets and steaks protected from direct contact with the ice with sheets of shiny paper. Go to a store that's popular so there's a lot of turnover. If you're buying fillets, avoid buying a small tail piece, especially if you see a bunch of tail pieces in the case, left over from the better cuts. If I have any doubts about the freshness of the fish—fillets or steaks with a dull or matte look instead of a sheen—I ask for a whole piece of center-cut fillet or even a whole fillet (much of the time forcing them to fillet a new fish) and cut it up myself when I get it home. If you buy your fish and have any doubts, immediately open the package (I do this while hiding behind a shelf of canned goods) and give it a sniff. If it smells fishy, take it back.

Storing: Ideally you should eat salmon the day you buy it (or soon after you catch it), but if you need to store it for a day or two (for periods up to 3 months you can freeze it tightly wrapped in plastic wrap and then aluminum foil) you need to take a few precautions. The idea is to keep the salmon as near the freezing point as possible without letting it get in direct contact with ice. Unless you have a giant freezer or a limitless supply of ice to keep filling your bathtub, a whole salmon is almost impossible to store. If you end up with one, fillet it to make storing easier. Wrap whole fillets tightly in plastic wrap and seal steaks or fillet pieces in resealable bags and nestle them in ice. To prevent the fish from coming in contact with melted ice, put ice in a colander set over a bowl in the refrigerator and nestle in the wrapped fish so it's buried in the ice.

Gutting: If you've caught your own salmon or have a generous friend, you may have to gut the salmon yourself. To do this, notice the small anal opening on the bottom of the salmon about ¼ the length of the fish away from the tail. Insert a sharp knife into this opening and slide the blade up along the belly all the way to the base of the head. Stick the knife into the belly just deep enough to cut through it—not deeper or you'll cut up the viscera and make the job needlessly messy. Reach into the belly opening and pull out the viscera, cutting with a sharp knife the membranes that hold the viscera attached to the rest of the fish. Rinse out the inside of the salmon.

Removing the Gills: Because gills collect dirt and grit, they are often removed. You only have to worry about this if you're cooking a whole salmon or using the head, such as for the red wine sauce on page 35. The fish seller will usually do it for you in a shop, but if you've caught your own fish, after gutting it, use heavy kitchen shears to cut through the base of the head where the two hard pieces of cartilage on each side of the salmon's head join at the bottom. At this point it will be easy to see the pink or red gills. Cut along the gills where they join the fish while tugging at them with your fingers and the whole gill section should come out.

Scaling: This is only necessary if you're cooking a whole salmon or if you're cooking salmon fillets or steaks with the skin on. They should do this for you at the fish store, but if you're stuck with a salmon with scales don't worry. Salmon scales are attached very loosely to the skin and are easy to remove. I scale fish outside or in a clear plastic bag so I don't end up with scales all over the kitchen. A fish scaler—cheap and easy to find at a cooking supply store— makes scaling easy. Just move it along the length of the fish. I work in both directions but it's most important to apply pressure as you're working from head to tail. If you don't have a fish scaler, scrape off the scales with the back of a knife instead. As the scales come off, the salmon will loose some of its sheen, but you should also run your fingers all over it to feel for any patches you may have missed. Rinse the salmon with the garden hose or in the sink.

Filleting: Since filleting can be a little tricky, you're usually better off buying your salmon already filleted. But one way of making sure your salmon is fresh is to buy a whole one—the whole ones at the fish market are likely to be the freshest—and fillet it yourself. Of course you can always ask them to do this at the fish market but you might have to put up with a certain amount of indignation.

There are two ways to fillet a salmon. The classic method, used for most round fish, is to cut along the base of the head and then slide the knife along the back, flush with the backbone. I find this the more difficult of the two methods because it's easy to lose your place and cut into flesh. But if you've done it before or you're used to filleting fish, go ahead and do what you know best. Whichever method you do use, remember to slide the knife in only one direction—don't move it back and forth. Try to make long slices instead of little jagged ones—or the fillet will look ragged. The second method involves boning the salmon, starting through the stomach. Both the methods described below assume you are right-handed.

Back Method: Set the salmon running horizontally in front of you with the head facing to the left. Slide a sharp boning knife or fish-filleting knife (these are flexible) under the base of the head, just behind where the gills were. Face the knife at an angle toward the head so that you leave as little of the fillet attached to the head as possible. Cut all the way down to the bone—until you can't cut any farther.

Move the salmon so its head is away from you, its tail is closest to you, and its back is to your right. Slide the knife along the back of the salmon, cutting only about ½ inch in until you reach the tail. Starting again at the base of the head, slide the knife in somewhat deeper until you find the backbone. (This is the tricky part since salmon backbones don't go all the way out to the edge of the fish.) Once you find the backbone, slide the knife back, again toward the tail, keeping the front part of the knife flush and on top of the backbone. Now that you have the backbone as a guide, slide the knife flush along the backbone while pulling back the top fillet with your left hand. Continue following bone—as long as you're not cutting through flesh or bone but are just following along the bone you won't have any problem—until you come to the ribs. You can cut through the ribs and remove them later, but I find it easier to follow them, keeping the knife against them, until I reach the ends of the belly flaps. Continue in this way until you've completely removed the top fillet.

You now will be left with the bottom fillet with the head, backbones, and ribs attached (see page 10). Leaving the fillet with the bones facing up, slide the knife under the bones—again starting at the base of the head— and slide the knife under the backbone, keeping the knife flush with the underside of the bones while pressing against the top of the bones with the palm of your left hand to keep the bones firmly against the knife. Continue in this way until you completely detach the backbone and head from the bottom fillet. Trim off the small strip of bones that runs along the upper side of each fillet.

Stomach Method: Make a diagonal cut at the base of the salmon's head in the same way described in the previous method. Make a crosswise slit at the top of the tail—just where the flesh starts—and then slide the knife up from the tail along the belly side of the salmon, keeping the knife flush against the bone, until you reach the belly opening. Fold back one of the salmon's stomach flaps as best you can. With a boning knife or small chefs' knife—don't use a flexible knife at this stage—cut through the top row of ribs where they join the backbone. You may have to use a quick jerking motion because the bones are somewhat hard to cut through. Don't let the knife penetrate behind the bones or you'll cut into flesh. When you've cut through all the bones, switch to a flexible knife and slide up the length of the salmon, starting from the tail end and working up to the head and keeping the knife flat and flush against the backbone so you don't cut into any flesh. Fold back the top fillet as you go and remove it completely.

Removing pin bones with a pair of flat-ended fish tweezers.

Remove the bones from the bottom fillet by cutting through the rib bones where they join the backbone using the same method you used for the top fillet. Slide the knife under the backbone, keeping it parallel and flush against the backbones by pressing gently on the backbone with your left hand. When you've removed the backbone you'll have two fillets with only the ribs attached. Remove the ribs by sliding the flexible knife under them and pressing down on the bones with the palm of your left hand to keep them flush against the knife blade. Remove the ribs from both fillets. Trim off the strip of bones that runs along the upper side of the top fillet.

Cutting Whole Salmon into Steaks: Unless you've caught your own salmon, it is unlikely you'll have to do this yourself. When cutting a salmon into steaks, keep in mind that all you're doing is slicing it crosswise.

Cut diagonally under the base of the head on both sides of the salmon. Snap the head back and remove it. Slice the salmon crosswise with the heaviest chefs' knife you have. The thickness of each steak is up to you. When you get down to the backbone, give the back of the knife a whack with a rolling pin, mallet, or hammer with a towel wrapped around it until you feel the knife break through the bone. Continue slicing with the chefs' knife until you cut off the steak.

Skinning: To remove the skin from salmon fillets, set the fillet on a cutting board, skin side down, with the tail facing you. Slide a flexible knife between the flesh and the skin on the tail end until you've separated about an inch of skin from the flesh. Grip the flap of skin between the thumb and forefinger of your left hand—use a kitchen towel if it's slippery—and press down on the skin with a flexible knife held at a very small angle so that the knife is almost flat and flush against the skin. Pull on the skin with your left hand while moving it back and forth, side to side. Move the knife very slightly with your right hand to keep it flush with the skin but most of the movement should be made with the skin, not the knife. Keep pulling and moving back and forth until the whole skin just pulls off. Turn the fillet over to see if you've left any patches of skin attached. If you have, slide a sharp knife under the skin and remove the skin by sliding the knife under with the blade facing upward at a gentle angle so you don't cut into flesh.

Removing Pin Bones from Fillets and Steaks: If you slide your fingers along the flesh side of a fillet or along the side of a salmon steak (except those cut near the tail) you'll feel tiny bones, called pin bones, sticking out. These are easiest to remove with needle-nose pliers, but a pair of tweezers (they sell special kinds of flat-ended tweezers at kitchen supply stores for this job) or even a thumbnail and forefinger will do the trick. Pin bones are easiest to remove from fillets that have had their skin removed so if you're skinning your fillets, do that first. To remove the pin bones from fillets, try to pull them straight out—they point at an angle toward where the head was—instead of pulling them backwards, which tears the flesh. Pin bones only run along the two-thirds of the fillet nearest the head. To remove pin bones from steaks, feel for them with your fingers and pull them out in the same way.

Cutting and Sectioning Salmon for Even Cooking: Salmon is sometimes hard to cook evenly because of its shape. You'll see that the whole fillet tapers and grows thinner near the tail and that the fillet also thins out along the belly flaps. If you look at salmon steaks, unless they're cut from the tail end, you'll see the belly flaps hanging down. Because the belly flaps are thinner, they inevitably cook faster. To make sure that salmon steaks cook evenly, convert them into medallions (see page 20) by removing their bones and tying them into rounds, something that sounds harder to do than it is.

Cutting fillets into pieces of even thickness is a little trickier. The ideal approach is to cut the salmon fillet lengthwise in half and cut the thick side into thick individual pieces for cooking. It's unlikely that they'll do this for you at the fish store, but you can do it at home and freeze the belly flaps for salmon tartare (see page 117), ravioli (see page 151), or samosas (see page 86). If you're baking individual pieces of salmon fillet, you can solve the thickness problem by cutting the fillet crosswise into individual servings and then folding under the belly flap. You can also slice the fillet into escalopes (see below). Another method for getting equal-size pieces out of an unevenly shaped fillet is to cut it lengthwise down the middle and cut the thick side into pieces with smaller dimensions (but the same weight) as pieces from the thin side. You will of course need to adjust the cooking times since the thinner pieces will cook faster—but at least everyone will get the same amount of salmon.

Tying Salmon Steaks into Medallions: To make salmon steaks easier to eat and to ensure that they cook evenly, remove their bones and tie them up with string. This is easiest with steaks that are at least ¾ inch thick—if they're thinner the string will come off.

To prepare medallions, first remove any pin bones from the sides of the steaks with pliers or tweezers. Slide a small paring knife along the inside of the belly flaps, between the flesh and the ribs, keeping the knife flush against the bones so you don't cut into the flesh. Do this to both of the flaps. Cut along one side of the backbone all the way up to, but not through, the skin on top of the salmon steak, originally the salmon's back. Keep the knife flush against the backbone. Get as close to the skin as you can without cutting through it. Cut the backbone away from the inside of the skin. Repeat this on the other side of the backbone. At this point you'll have completely boned the steak, which should consist of two tapering flaps held together by a small piece of skin. Trim off about 2 inches of skin from the end of one of the flaps, keeping the knife pointed against the skin so you don't lose any flesh. Fold this skinless flap into the inside of the steak and wrap the other flap around it so you end up with a perfect round. Tie the round with a double loop of string. Make sure the string is tight enough to hold the medallion together but not too tight or the medallion will push its way out of the string as it cooks.

Cutting Salmon Fillets into Escalopes: The word *escalope* is French for what in English is technically a scallop but because "salmon scallops" sounds ridiculous, I've stuck with the French.

An escalope is simply a relatively thin slice of just about anything. Cutting large pieces or whole salmon fillets into escalopes has the advantage of allowing you to control how thick the slices are. It takes a little practice and a thin flexible knife, but most of the technique can be learned just using common sense. Depending on the dish, escalopes can be from about ⅛ inch thick (the fillet is sliced in the same way as smoked salmon) to ½ inch thick, depending on the recipe. Escalopes are best for sautéing, broiling or baking—they are too thin and fragile for grilling.

To cut a salmon fillet into escalopes, first remove any pin bones and then decide how thick you want the escalopes and the size you want them to be when you serve them. Because of salmon's irregular shape, you may end up with some odd-sized pieces but you can piece these together on the plate. If you're buying a whole fillet or a large piece, be sure that the skin is attached to make the salmon easier to work with. If you have a tail end piece, start 4 or 5 inches up from the end and cut at an angle anywhere from ⅛ inch to ½ inch (but usually about ¼ inch) into the salmon. Hold your left hand over the part of the salmon you're going to slice and slide the knife toward the tail, keeping the escalope the same thickness. Continue slicing in this way, working back along the fillet, starting about an inch up toward the head for each slice and continue to make escalopes, following the contours of your first slice so the escalopes all end up the same thickness. As the fillet gets thicker, you can just cut deeper into the fish as you're slicing, without moving back. As you approach the head end of the fillet—or if you're working with a head end piece—the slicing becomes slightly problematic because the fillet isn't the same thickness so you'll end up with small pieces from the thick end, and the escalopes will get wider as you get farther down into the fillet and closer to the skin. Because this is almost impossible to avoid, I don't worry about the sizes of the pieces but just piece them together on the plate. I aim for escalopes that measure between 4 and 6 inches on each side.

A Note on Serving Sizes: Most of us eat and serve salmon as a main course and are happy with a 6- to 8-ounce portion, but many of the salmon dishes given here also make great first courses for more elaborate dinners. If you're serving salmon as a first course or a light luncheon course, just decrease the serving sizes to about 4 ounces.

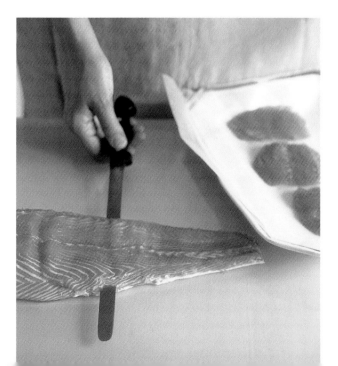

Slicing salmon fillet into escalopes.

SAUTÉING

There are several advantages to sautéing salmon versus using other techniques. First, it's quick; second, it leaves the outside of the fillet, steak, medallion, or escalope with a slightly crisp and brown outer coating; and last, you can make a simple sauce or glaze in a couple of minutes in the pan you used for sautéing.

To sauté successfully you need a to preheat a heavy-bottomed pan with a little bit of oil or clarified butter in it before putting in the pieces of salmon. It's important that the pan be as hot as possible—but not so hot that it will burn whatever cooking fat you're using—before you add the salmon. If the salmon starts to brown too quickly, or even burn, you can always turn the heat down once the salmon's surface is browned. If you sauté at too low a temperature, the salmon will never brown, or even worse, it will release juices and boil instead of forming a crust. The salmon pieces should be dry before you put them in the pan, again to help them brown. Cooks often make the mistake of seasoning the salmon with salt and pepper several minutes before sautéing, which draws moisture out of the fish and makes it wet. When seasoning 30 minutes to 4 hours ahead of time—something I recommend since it allows the flavor of the salt and pepper to penetrate into the fish—be sure to pat the fish dry with a paper towel before putting it in the pan. Otherwise, sprinkle the salmon with salt and pepper *immediately* before putting it in the pan. An even better method, which firms up the salmon and makes it less likely to stick, is to soak thin pieces of salmon in brine for an hour and thicker pieces for 2 hours and then pat them dry and season them with pepper just before sautéing (see page 93).

I prefer heavy nonstick pans for sautéing most fish because fish, especially with the skin on, loves to stick. In a pinch, I use a well-seasoned cast-iron skillet. Avoid non-anodized aluminum; it causes fish to stick unless you use oil heated until it's smoking hot, which can give the salmon an unpleasant taste. When you first set the pieces of salmon into the hot pan, give the pan a quick back-and-forth shake so the surface of the salmon cooks a tiny bit, making it less likely to stick.

If you're sautéing salmon fillets, you need to decide whether or not to leave the skin on. Since sautéing skin-on salmon fillets turns the skin delightfully crispy and juicy, I always leave the skin on, but if your guests or family are squeamish about skin, buy fillets with the skin off. If you do decide to sauté skin-on fillets, make sure the skin has been perfectly de-scaled by running your fingers along the skin and seeing if any scales come off. If they do, don't worry. Salmon scales are very easy to take off—just rub the skin back and forth with the back of a knife and then rinse off the scales. Keep in mind that salmon skin shrinks as soon as it gets hot, which can cause the salmon fillet to curl so that the concave part doesn't touch the pan and the skin doesn't brown evenly. To avoid this, put the fillets in the hot pan, skin side down, and, after giving the pan a quick little shake, press on the top of the fillets with the back of a spatula to keep the skin in contact with the pan. When cooking skin-on filets, it's usually best to sauté them longer on the skin side—giving the skin time to release its fat and turn crispy—than on the flesh side. If you're sautéing fillets that are thinner on one end than the other, before sautéing fold the thinner end—the belly flap—under so the fillet ends up an even thickness.

SAUTÉED SALMON FILLETS OR STEAKS

MAKES 4 MAIN-COURSE OR FIRST-COURSE SERVINGS

four 6- to 8-ounce salmon fillets with the skin on or off, steaks, or medallions (see pages 18 and 20) for main courses, or **four 4-ounce escalopes** (see page 20) for first-course servings

salt (or ½ recipe brine, see page 93)

pepper

1 tablespoon olive oil or clarified butter

Season the salmon liberally on both sides with salt and pepper and let sit in the refrigerator for between 30 minutes and 4 hours, or soak it in brine in the refrigerator for 1 to 2 hours, depending on its thickness. Place a plate on top of the salmon to keep it submerged. In either case, pat the salmon dry just before sautéing. If you've used brine, season it only with pepper.

Heat the oil or butter in a heavy-bottomed (preferably nonstick) sauté pan just large enough to hold the salmon, until the oil forms ripples and barely begins to smoke.

If you're sautéing skin-on fillets, place them in the pan skin side down and press on them firmly for the first 2 minutes with the back of a spatula to keep the fillet from curling. If you're sautéing skin-off fillets, put the most attractive side down—the side that was facing the inside of the salmon, not the side that once had the skin attached—in the pan first (so that it will be facing up when you turn the fillets over). For inch-thick fillets or steaks, sauté over high heat for 3 to 5 minutes on the first side, turn them over with a spatula, and sauté for 2 to 3 minutes on the second side. If the salmon starts to brown or the oil or butter smokes, turn the heat down to medium. Keep in mind that the total cooking time should be 8 to 10 minutes per inch of total thickness (depending on how you like your salmon done) and that the salmon should spend more time sautéing on the first side (the eventual presentation side) so that you're sure to end up with a savory golden crust or crisp skin. Adjust the cooking times according to the salmon's thickness.

Remove the salmon from the pan with a spatula and pat it dry on both sides with a paper towel to get rid of any taste of burned fat. Serve immediately on hot plates.

SAUTÉED SALMON "SALTIMBOCCA"

Saltimbocca, a dish popular in Rome, is made from thin slices of veal each covered with a thin slice of prosciutto and a leaf or two of fresh sage. I cook the same dish with salmon, cut into scallopini (escalopes) like the veal.

MAKES 4 LIGHT MAIN-COURSE OR FIRST-COURSE SERVINGS

4 salmon escalopes (see page 20), about ½ inch thick
   and 5 inches on each side (about 4 ounces each)
pepper
4 thin (but not paper-thin) slices prosciutto,
   each slice large enough to cover an escalope
8 fresh sage leaves
6 tablespoons butter
¼ cup dry white wine

Season the escalopes with pepper. Trim the prosciutto slices so they are the exact size as the salmon slices and place a slice on top of each piece of salmon. Place 2 sage leaves on top of the prosciutto and slide a toothpick or wooden skewer through the leaf—thread it so it goes through each leaf, the prosciutto and the salmon in 2 places. (You'll need 2 toothpicks per escalope.) Sauté the slices, prosciutto side down first, in a nonstick or well-seasoned pan in 2 tablespoons of butter for about 2 minutes. Make sure the pan is hot and the butter frothy before you add the salmon, and give the pan a little shake as soon as you put in the escalopes to keep them from sticking. Turn them over gently with a long spatula and cook for about 30 seconds on the second side. Transfer the salmon to heated plates and gently pull out the toothpicks. If the salmon is too hot to handle, pull the toothpicks out with a small pair of pliers.

Pour the burned butter out of the sauté pan and add the remaining butter. Heat over medium heat until it barely begins to brown, add the white wine, and boil for about 1 minute. Spoon the sauce over the salmon and serve.

TERIYAKI-GLAZED SALMON FILLETS

As delicious as a plain piece of sautéed salmon can be, salmon has such a full flavor that it lends itself to all sorts of variations. One method—glazing—is easy to pull off by adding flavorful liquids to the still-hot sauté pan after removing the salmon, boiling the liquids down to a glaze, and then putting the salmon back in the pan for a few seconds on each side to coat it. One of my favorites is teriyaki glaze made with soy sauce and mirin (a kind of syrupy sweet sake) or, if I don't have mirin, a little sugar. The teriyaki treatment is best with skin-on fillets.

MAKES 4 MAIN-COURSE SERVINGS

four 6- to 8-ounce salmon fillets with the skin on
freshly ground pepper
1 tablespoon peanut oil or olive oil
¼ cup naturally brewed Japanese soy sauce
3 tablespoons mirin or 1 tablespoon granulated sugar
   dissolved in 2 tablespoons boiling water

Rub the salmon skin with your fingers. If any scales rub off, gently scrape the skin with the back of a knife and rinse the salmon under cold water. Pat it dry with paper towels. Season lightly with pepper and refrigerate until you're ready to sauté.

Heat the oil or butter in a heavy-bottomed (preferably nonstick) sauté pan just large enough to hold the salmon until the oil ripples and barely begins to smoke. Pat the salmon dry with a paper towel. Place the salmon fillets in the pan skin side down, give the pan a quick little shake, and press on them firmly for the first 2 minutes of sautéing with the back of a spatula to keep the skin in contact with the hot oil and to prevent curling. Sauté the salmon over high heat for about 4 minutes—until the skin is lightly brown and crispy. Turn the fillets over with a spatula and sauté them for 30 seconds to 2 minutes on the second side, depending on the thickness of the fillets. If the salmon starts to brown or the oil or butter smokes, turn the heat down to medium. While the total cooking time should be 8 to 10 minutes per inch of total thickness (depending on how you like your salmon done), keep in mind that it's going to spend another 2 minutes in the pan for the final glazing—so leave it a tad underdone.

Use a spatula to transfer the salmon to a plate covered with a triple layer of paper towels. Pat the top of the salmon with a paper towel to absorb any burned fat.

Pour the burned fat out of the sauté pan and wipe out any remaining fat with a paper towel. If the bottom of the pan has any burned juices clinging to it (which would make the glaze bitter), put about ¼ cup of water into it while it's still hot. Pour out the water and wipe the pan clean with a paper towel.

Pour the soy sauce and mirin (or sugar syrup) into the pan and boil the mixture over high heat for about 1 minute, until it looks syrupy. Don't overdo it or the glaze will burn. Turn the heat down to medium and return the salmon fillets to the pan, skin side down. Move them around in the pan so the skin is well coated with the glaze. After about 30 seconds, turn them over with a spatula and move them around for about 30 seconds more, with the flesh side facing down. Transfer them to hot plates and serve immediately.

MAPLE SYRUP AND MUSTARD-GLAZED SALMON FILLETS

Prepare the Teriyaki-Glazed Salmon Fillets, but instead of using soy sauce and mirin, stir together 3 tablespoons Dijon mustard with 2 tablespoons maple syrup and 2 tablespoon of water. Use this mixture as you would the soy sauce-mirin mixture in the teriyaki recipe, except do not boil down the glaze before putting the fillets back in the pan. Return the fillets to the pan immediately after stirring in the glaze.

HERB-CRUSTED SAUTÉED SALMON
FILLETS WITH PISTOU

Pistou is the southern French version of Genoa's *pesto*. Pesto is made with basil and garlic but also contains pine nuts, sometimes walnuts, and usually Parmigiano Reggiano. Pistou, a mixture often dolloped into vegetable soup, usually contains neither cheese nor nuts but frequently contains tomatoes. Purists insist that pistou (and pesto) be made by hand in a large mortar, but most of us don't have a mortar, much less one large enough to do the job efficiently. So I give in and use a blender. The herb crust has an assertive flavor of its own that matches that of the pistou. I don't combine the tomatoes with the pureed basil because they turn the basil a rather dull green—I add them to the dish separately. The egg yolk is optional. It turns the basil mixture into a very light mayonnaise and helps hold it together, but if you don't mind seeing little oil droplets in the basil mixture or you're worried about raw egg yolks, just leave it out. In this recipe the basil leaves are quickly blanched, which keeps the pistou a bright green and softens its flavor somewhat. Pistou made with unblanched leaves will taste fine but takes on a murky gray color.

MAKES 6 MAIN-COURSE SERVINGS

six 6- to 8-ounce salmon fillets with the skin and pin bones removed
   (fillets should be no more than 1 inch thick or herb coating will burn
   before fish is cooked)
salt (or ½ recipe brine, see page 93)
pepper
6 tablespoons total of fresh or dried chopped herbs such as thyme,
   marjoram, oregano, savory, or rosemary, alone or in combination
2 tablespoons olive oil

For the pistou:
2 tablespoons salt
leaves from 1 large bunch basil (about 1 tightly packed cup),
   washed and spun dry
2 cloves garlic, chopped fine and crushed to a paste with
   the side of a chefs' knife
1 egg yolk (optional)
½ cup extra-virgin olive oil
salt
pepper
4 medium tomatoes, peeled, seeded, chopped fine, or two cups
   assorted cherry tomatoes, quartered

Season the salmon liberally on both sides with salt and pepper and let sit in the refrigerator for between 30 minutes and 4 hours. You can also soak the salmon for 2 hours in brine (see page 93) and add the pepper just before sautéing. Pat dry, season with pepper only if you've used brine, and sprinkle the top and bottom with the chopped herbs. Press the herbs onto the salmon to help them adhere. Keep in the refrigerator until you're ready to sauté.

Make the pistou within an hour of cooking the salmon—if made sooner it will lose color. Bring 2 quarts of water to a rapid boil with 2 tablespoons salt, plunge in the basil leaves, and stir them around with a wooden spoon, leaving them in the water for no more than 2 seconds. Drain in a colander and immediately cool by rinsing with cold water. Combine the basil, garlic, ½ cup of water, and the optional egg yolk in a blender and puree for 1 minute, until smooth. Transfer the basil mixture to a bowl and gently work in the olive oil with a wooden spoon. Season to taste with salt and pepper. (If you don't use an egg yolk, the oil will form small droplets within the green basil puree. This is fine—some people find it more attractive—but an egg yolk will ensure a sauce that's perfectly homogeneous.)

Just before sautéing the salmon, gently heat the pistou mixture in a saucepan while stirring. Don't allow the pistou mixture to come to a boil, especially if you've used an egg yolk, which will scramble.

Sauté the salmon fillets, pat them with a paper towel to eliminate fat—be careful not to rub off the herbs—and transfer them to heated plates. Wipe out the hot sauté pan, and add in the chopped tomatoes, stirring them just long enough to warm them. Ladle the pistou over and around each piece of salmon and spoon the warmed tomatoes over just before serving.

Jerked foods are usually cooked slowly in a covered barbecue so they absorb the smoky flavor of the smoldering wood, but because I don't always have the energy, or it's too cold to fire up the barbecue, I've adapted the traditional technique so I can sauté the salmon in a nonstick pan. Jerked salmon is best made with thick fillets or medallions. Thyme is the predominant flavor in most jerk rubs or marinades. I prefer to use less, so the flavor of the other ingredients—the spices and ginger—are easier to taste.

MAKES 6 MAIN-COURSE SERVINGS

six 6- to 8-ounce thick salmon fillets with the
skin removed, steaks, or medallions (see page 20)
3 tablespoons olive oil

For the jerk marinade:
2 scotch bonnet or habanero chilies or 4 serrano chilies
3 tablespoons chopped fresh thyme leaves or 2 tablespoons dried
1 small red onion, peeled and chopped
3 cloves garlic, chopped fine and crushed to a paste
with the side of a chefs' knife
2 imported bay leaves (California bay leaves have an aggressive
eucalyptus flavor), chopped
3 tablespoons finely grated fresh ginger
½ teaspoon ground nutmeg
2 teaspoons ground allspice
2 tablespoons ground coriander (this is best when you grind it
yourself in a clean coffee grinder)
1 teaspoon ground cinnamon
½ teaspoon ground cloves
¼ cup lime juice (from 1 or 2 limes)
2 tablespoons Japanese soy sauce
¼ cup peanut oil
1 teaspoon freshly ground black pepper
2 teaspoons salt

Rub the salmon with a tablespoon of olive oil and refrigerate while you're making the marinade.

I'm usually cavalier about chopping chilies without gloves on but the chilies in jerk marinade are so hot that I highly recommend wearing gloves. Cut off the stems, cut the chilies vertically in half and whack each half against the cutting board to get rid of most of the seeds. Chop the chilies and combine them with the thyme, onion, garlic, bay leaves, ginger, nutmeg, allspice, coriander, cinnamon, cloves, lime juice, soy sauce, peanut oil, and salt and pepper in a food processor or blender. Puree the mixture for 30 seconds to a minute. Smear the marinade on both sides of the salmon and refrigerate for 4 to 12 hours.

When you're ready to sauté, rub off the marinade—a little left clinging does no harm—and heat the remaining 2 tablespoons olive oil in a nonstick pan until it begins to ripple but doesn't smoke. Cook a 1-inch thick piece of salmon for about 4 minutes on each side. I like to serve jerked salmon with a refreshing salsa such as the cucumber salsa on page 69 or the tropical fruit salsa on page 71.

Sauces for Salmon Fillets, Steaks, Medallions, or Escalopes

Once you've sautéed a few pieces of salmon, it's easy to make a sauce in the pan—what professionals call "pan-deglazed" sauces—as soon as you take the salmon out of the pan. To make salmon with a sauce, sauté the salmon following the basic recipe on page 25, pour out any of the hot fat used for cooking the salmon—you don't want it to end up in your sauce—and wipe the pan out with a paper towel. Make sure that any juices released by the salmon into the pan haven't burned. If they have, rinse out the pan with a little water to get rid of them before adding the ingredients for a sauce. Using the pan you used for sautéing the salmon for making a pan-deglazed sauce then becomes simply a matter of convenience and saves you from dirtying another dish. Virtually any pan-deglazed sauce can be made ahead of time in another pan, but unless you're cooking for a crowd, it's rarely worth the trouble.

SAUTÉED SALMON FILLETS
WITH RED WINE SAUCE

The trick to this rather luxurious dish is to make an intensely flavored but light-textured red wine sauce out of a couple of salmon heads, and then use the sauce to surround sautéed salmon fillets. Making the sauce takes some time but most of the work can be done ahead.

MAKES 6 MAIN-COURSE SERVINGS

six 6- to 8-ounce salmon fillets with the skin on or off

For the red wine sauce:
2 salmon heads
1 large onion, peeled and chopped coarse
1 carrot, peeled and chopped coarse
6-inch length celery, chopped
3 garlic cloves, crushed
10 sprigs fresh thyme or 1 teaspoon dried
2 imported bay leaves
2 tablespoons olive oil
6 cups red wine
1 small bunch parsley
4 tablespoons cold, unsalted butter
2 teaspoons good quality red wine vinegar, or more to taste
2 tablespoons finely chopped parsley
salt
pepper

Ask the fish seller to cut the gills out of the salmon heads. If you buy heads at the supermarket and they still have their gills, cut the gills out by turning the heads over and using heavy shears to cut the gills out of each side of the heads. Discard the gills and soak the heads for 30 minutes in cold water.

Put the onion, carrot, celery, garlic, thyme, bay leaves, and olive oil in a 4-quart pot and add the drained salmon heads. Cook over medium heat for about 30 minutes, stirring every few minutes with a wooden spoon while scraping caramelized juices off the bottom of the pot, until the vegetables have browned, the heads have completely fallen apart, and the bottom of the pot is coated with a layer of oily fat from the salmon. (The concoction is going to look very unappetizing at this point—don't worry.) Add one cup of red wine to the pot and turn the heat on high. Use a wooden spoon to stir the mixture, scraping against the bottom and sides of the pot to dissolve the brown (and flavorful) glaze until all the wine has evaporated, again just leaving a layer of oily fat. Watch closely so you don't overdo it and burn the bottom of the pan. Add the rest of the wine and the bunch of parsley and simmer the mixture gently over low to medium heat for 30 minutes.

Strain the broth through a fine mesh strainer into a saucepan and simmer over medium heat, using a ladle to skim off any froth or fat that floats to the top, until you're left with about 1½ cups of concentrated broth. Strain into a small bowl and refrigerate overnight, covered with plastic wrap. If you're in a hurry, set the bowl in another bowl containing ice. When the broth has set and the fat on top has congealed, scrape the fat off with a spoon and discard it. You should end up with about a cup of concentrated fat-free red wine base for making your sauce.

Sauté the salmon fillets as described in the recipe on page 25. Bring the concentrated salmon broth to a gentle simmer in a small saucepan and whisk in the butter, vinegar, chopped parsley, and salt and pepper to taste. If the sauce tastes flat, add a tiny bit more vinegar. Place the sautéed salmon fillets in the center of heated soup plates—skin side up if you've left the skin on, skin side down if you removed it—and ladle the sauce over and around the salmon.

Variations: Salmon fillets with red wine sauce look and taste great when topped with sautéed mushrooms (either cultivated or wild); glazed pearl onions, baby carrots, or turnips; French-style thin string beans boiled until tender, about 7 minutes; baby peas, or fava beans. These ingredients can be used alone or in combination.

I've never encountered salmon with mole sauce, although I do remember a delicious mole made with shrimp, tasted on a trip to Mexico. Because mole sauce can be made independently of whatever you're serving it with, you can make it several days ahead (or freeze it for up to several months) and heat it at the last minute when you've cooked the salmon. Most people associate mole sauces with chocolate, which is used in small amounts in some versions, but moles get most of their character from dried chilies, spices, and sometimes ground peanuts. If you can't find all the chilies listed below, just use more of one or two of the others. If you find yourself making moles often—an easy habit to fall into—experiment with different chilies (see sources on page 156 for where to buy dried chilies).

MAKES 8 MAIN-COURSE SERVINGS

eight 6- to 8-ounce salmon steaks or fillets with the skin on or off

salt (or ½ recipe brine, see page 93)

pepper

4 dried ancho chilies

2 dried mulato chilies

2 dried guajillo chilies

1 tablespoon butter, olive oil, or corn oil

1 medium onion, peeled and chopped

2 large cloves garlic, chopped

1 teaspoon fresh thyme leaves or ½ teaspoon dried

½ teaspoon dried oregano (preferably Mexican), chopped fine

2 medium tomatoes, stemmed and chopped coarse

1 cup chicken broth or water (or more as needed to thin sauce at the end)

¼ teaspoon ground cloves

1 teaspoon ground cinnamon

⅔ cup white raisins, 3 tablespoons reserved for sauce,
   the rest soaked in enough water to barely cover

3 tablespoons peanut butter (all natural—contents should read "peanuts, salt" only)

juice of ½ lime or more to taste

salt

1 tablespoon olive oil, for sautéing the salmon

3 tablespoons pumpkin seeds or slivered almonds, toasted for 15 minutes in a 300° F oven, (optional)

1 cup sour cream

Season the salmon liberally on both sides with salt and pepper and let sit in the refrigerator for between 30 minutes and 4 hours. You can also soak the salmon for 2 hours in brine (see page 93) and add the pepper just before sautéing. Pat dry and season with pepper if you've used brine just before sautéing.

Wipe the dust off the chilies with a damp towel and toast them in a hot skillet. Heat the skillet over high heat for about 3 minutes and put in the chilies. Turn them around every few seconds with a pair of tongs until you smell their fragrance, after about a minute. Cut off the stems, cut the chilies in half lengthwise, and rinse out their seeds under cold running water. Put the chilies in a bowl with just enough warm water to cover, until they are soft and pliable, about 30 minutes. Discard the soaking liquid. Chop coarse and reserve.

Heat the butter or oil in a medium saucepan. Add the onion and garlic and stir over medium heat, using a wooden spoon, until the onion turns translucent, about 10 minutes. Add the thyme and oregano and stir for 2 minutes more. Add the tomatoes, the broth or water, and the chilies and bring to a very gentle simmer. Simmer, covered, for 15 to 20 minutes, to infuse the flavor of the herbs and chilies. Add the cloves and cinnamon, the unsoaked raisins, and the peanut butter and simmer for 1 minute more. Put the sauce in a blender and puree it, starting out using quick pulses with the blender setting on low while holding the top firmly on the blender with a towel wrapped around the blender top to keep the hot sauce from shooting out. Gradually increase the speed and duration of the pulses and then puree the sauce on high for 1 minute. Add the lime juice—don't worry about the seeds—and work the sauce through a strainer with the back of a ladle or through a food mill. Season to taste with salt and, if necessary, more lime juice. If the sauce is too thick, thin it with additional broth or water.

Sauté the salmon in olive oil with the skin on or off—it's up to you—following the directions on page 25.

Heat the pumpkin seeds or almonds in a small pan. Heat the raisins in their soaking liquid in another small pan or in the microwave. Put the salmon on heated plates, cover with the mole sauce, and sprinkle over the drained raisins and pumpkin seeds or almonds. If you want to get fancy, cut a tiny piece out of the corner of a plastic bag, put in some sour cream, and squeeze it over the salmon in decorative streaks.

Pass the rest of the sour cream at the table for guests to help themselves.

PORCINI-COATED SALMON AND
WILD MUSHROOM EMULSION

You can make this recipe as simple or as complicated as you like. The simplest method is to coat salmon fillets on both sides with ground porcini mushrooms and sauté it in the usual way (see page 25). Or you can get sophisticated and serve the salmon with the morel emulsion (basically cream pureed with dried morels softened in a little water), and if you're really showing off, garnish the finished plates with sautéed wild mushrooms. When shopping for dried porcini, look for large slices that really look like the cross section of a mushroom—not little broken pieces. I always press my nose against the bag and smell—the mushroom fragrance should be so penetrating that you can smell it through the bag. It's hard to make a small amount of porcini dust—it won't twirl around in the blender—so make the amount given here, which may be more than you need, and freeze the rest. You can, of course, serve this dish as a main course, but it also makes a very elegant starter for a more elaborate meal. When I serve it as a first course, I cut the salmon into 4-ounce escalopes.

MAKES 4 MAIN-COURSE OR 8 FIRST-COURSE SERVINGS

**four 6- to 8-ounce salmon fillets, skin and pin bones removed, or eight
4-ounce salmon escalopes** (if you're serving the salmon as a first course)
salt (or ½ recipe brine, see page 93)
pepper
1 cup dried porcini (about 1 ounce)
2 tablespoons butter

For the optional morel emulsion:
1 cup dried morels (about 1 ounce)
1 cup heavy cream
salt
pepper

For the optional wild mushroom garniture:
1 pound assorted fresh wild mushrooms, such as morels, hedgehogs,
or chanterelles
2 tablespoons butter
salt
pepper
2 tablespoons chopped parsley

Season the salmon liberally on both sides with salt and pepper and let sit in the refrigerator for between 30 minutes and 4 hours, or soak it in brine in the refrigerator for 2 hours for 6- to 8-ounce escalopes or 1 hour for 4-ounce escalopes. Place a plate on top of the salmon to keep it submerged. Pat the salmon dry just before sautéing. If you've used brine, season it only with pepper.

If the porcini feel at all moist or flexible, dry them in a 200° F oven for 30 minutes until they feel hard and brittle. Puree them in a blender—make sure the blender is perfectly dry—on high speed for 1 minute. You should end up with about ¼ cup of porcini powder.

Making the Optional Morel Emulsion: Rinse the morels in a strainer under cold running water for few seconds and put them in a bowl with ⅓ cup warm water for 30 minutes. Stir them around in the bowl every 10 minutes so they soften and absorb the water evenly. Squeeze the liquid out of the morels—save it in the bowl—and put the morels in a saucepan with the heavy cream. Slowly pour any liquid left in the bowl into the saucepan, leaving any grit or sand behind in the bowl. Bring to a simmer. While the mixture is still hot, puree it in a blender and strain it back into the saucepan. Rinse the blender with ¼ cup of water and strain this with the rest of the mixture. Press hard on the strainer with a ladle to work some of the pureed mushrooms through to thicken the emulsion. While you're grilling or sautéing the salmon, bring the emulsion to the simmer—don't let the cream get thick (if it does, thin it with a little broth or water)—and season to taste with salt and pepper.

Preparing the Optional Mushroom Garniture: Just before you sauté the salmon, sauté the wild mushrooms for about 10 minutes in butter on medium to high heat. Season with salt and pepper, sprinkle with parsley, and sauté for 30 seconds more.

Sautéing and Finishing: Pat the salmon dry. Spread the porcini dust on a plate and coat the salmon on one or both sides and sauté the salmon in butter. If you're serving the salmon without the emulsion, just place it on heated plates. If you are using the emulsion, it's best to arrange the salmon in heated soup plates with rims and spoon the emulsion around. If you're using the wild mushrooms, spoon them over and around the salmon.

Serving Sautéed Salmon with Savory Broths

Even though sautéed salmon takes well to a sauce made in the pan, much of the time these sauces are held together with butter or cream, rich ingredients that some people avoid. Asian cooks and contemporary chefs often surround sautéed foods, including salmon, with savory broths instead of rich sauces. These broths can be as simple or as complicated as you like and can range from a simple clear broth infused with herbs to a more elaborate soup-like combination containing coconut milk (for a Thai- or Indonesian-style version) or miso (for a Japanese-style version) or homemade garlic and saffron mayonnaise (for a French-style version).

When serving sautéed salmon surrounded with a soup-like sauce, keep two things in mind. First, you'll need soup plates or wide bowls so there will be room for liquid to surround the salmon, and you'll have to add something to prop the salmon up slightly above the surrounding liquid so it doesn't over-cook as it's sitting in the bowl. Asian recipes often call for various sorts of noodles that do the job perfectly and also give substance to the dish, turning it into a meal. Both Asian and Western cooks may also use mounds of cooked vegetables such as spinach or Swiss chard or bread slices—bread slices first sautéed in a little olive oil so they don't turn soggy when surrounded with liquid.

Dried porcini mushrooms.

SAUTÉED SALMON SERVED LIKE
A BOUILLABAISSE

The secret to southern French soups like bouillabaisse is whisking a pungent, garlicky sauce into a fish soup made with baby fish too small to serve, or, in my version, a broth made from fish heads and bones. Salmon bones and heads make a great red wine sauce (see page 35), but a fish broth made from salmon is too fishy. Since inexpensive fresh baby fish are hard to find in the United States, you can solve the problem by steaming open a couple of pounds of fresh mussels with some white wine and then combining the briny liquid they release with a homemade *aïoli* (garlic mayonnaise with olive oil). The aïoli can be made and the mussels steamed open earlier the same day you are serving the salmon.

MAKES 4 MAIN-COURSE SERVINGS

> **four 6- to 8-ounce medallions** (see page 20) **or salmon fillets**
> **with the skin on or off**
> salt
> pepper
> 1 tablespoon olive oil

For the aïoli:

> **1 small pinch saffron threads** (optional)
> **1 egg yolk**
> **1 teaspoon white wine vinegar**
> **½ teaspoon salt**
> **2 garlic cloves,** chopped fine
> **½ cup extra-virgin olive oil**

For the toasts:

> **four ½-inch thick slices of French country bread** about the same size
>   as each salmon fillet
> **4 tablespoons olive oil**

For the broth:

> **2 pounds mussels,** preferably small cultivated ones
> **1 cup dry white wine**
> **2 tablespoons chopped parsley**

Season the salmon fillets with salt and pepper and refrigerate them until you're ready to sauté.

To make the aïoli, combine the saffron threads with 1 tablespoon of water and reserve. Combine the egg yolk, vinegar, and salt in a small glass mixing bowl (metal bowls sometimes give the aïoli a metallic taste). Crush the chopped garlic with the side of a chefs' knife and add it to the egg yolk mixture. Work the olive oil into the mixture with a wooden spoon, adding the oil about a ½ teaspoon at a time and incorporating what you've added before adding more. When you've added about a third of the oil, start adding it a tablespoon at a time. Don't try making aïoli in a blender because the quick action of the blade, for some reason, turns extra-virgin olive oil bitter. Stir in the reserved saffron and its soaking liquid. Transfer the aïoli to a medium-size non-aluminum saucepan and reserve in a cool place, but not in the refrigerator, which can cause the aïoli to break.

Gently sauté the bread slices in 2 tablespoons of olive oil until they're brown on one side. Take the bread out of the pan, add 2 tablespoons more olive oil, and brown the bread slices on the other side. Reserve.

Use a stiff brush to scrub the mussels under cold running water. While you're scrubbing, push on the mussel shells, in opposing directions, so that any dead ones will come apart in your hand. Remove the beards if there are any. Pour the wine in a pot large enough to hold the mussels with some room left over (when they open they'll take up more room in the pot). Add the mussels, cover the pot, and cook over high heat for 5 minutes, until the wine comes to a rapid boil and all the mussels have opened. Turn off the heat, leave the lid on the pot and let rest for 2 minutes to finish cooking the mussels. Scoop the mussels into a bowl with a slotted spoon. Pull the top shell off each of the mussels and discard. Slowly pour the liquid—which should now be hot but not boiling from the mussel pot into the aïoli, leaving any grit behind in the pot. (Also add any liquid that has accumulated in the pot used to hold the mussels.) Add the chopped parsley and whisk the mixture together and reserve.

Heat the bread slices and soup plates in a low oven and sauté the salmon fillets as described in the recipe on page 25. Spread the mussels in a sauté pan and pour the aïoli mixture over them. Heat the pan over medium heat, shaking it back and forth, while gently moving the mussels around with a wooden spoon, to heat the liquid and the mussels. Don't let the liquid boil or it will curdle. Season to taste with pepper.

Place a toasted bread slice in the bottom of each bowl and place the fillets, skin side up, on top of the bread. If you've removed the skin, the skin side of the salmon often has an unsightly gray coloration. Because of this, present the salmon with the other side—the side that was facing the backbone—up. Ladle the broth and mussels around the salmon and serve immediately.

SAUTÉED SALMON WITH THAI-STYLE
COCONUT BROTH

The great thing about Thai-flavored broths is that you don't need to start with fish or chicken broth because the ingredients are so full of flavor that you can use water. In some parts of the country, tracking down all the ingredients can be a bit of a nuisance (although they're easily mail-ordered—see sources, page 156—and keep for at least a year in the freezer), but once you have them on hand, making the broth is a snap. I like to put a mound of spinach in each bowl—not really authentic, but good—to prop up the salmon and keep it from overcooking. The Thai broth and the spinach can be prepared earlier the same day you are serving the salmon.

MAKES 6 MAIN-COURSE SERVINGS

six 6- to 8-ounce salmon fillets with the skin on or off
salt (or ½ recipe brine, see page 93)
pepper
1½ tablespoons peanut oil or olive oil, for sautéing the salmon

For the spinach:
salt
1 pound or two 10-ounce bunches fresh spinach, stems removed,
    leaves washed until no sand remains, or one 10-ounce bag pre-washed
    spinach leaves, washed once again.

For the Thai broth:
2 shallots or 1 small red onion, peeled and chopped fine
2 cloves garlic, chopped fine and crushed to a paste with
    the side of a chefs' knife
6 kaffir lime leaves or six 1- by ¼-inch strips lime zest
1 stalk lemon grass
four ⅛-inch thick slices galangal (available at Asian groceries), optional
4 Thai chilies or 4 jalapeño peppers, stemmed, halved, seeded,
    and chopped fine
one 15-ounce can coconut milk (preferably a brand from Thailand—
    don't use sweetened coconut milk used for making piña coladas)
¼ cup Thai fish sauce or more to taste
¼ cup lime juice (from 1 or 2 limes)
2 tablespoons coarsely chopped cilantro
salt (optional)

Season the salmon liberally on both sides with salt and pepper and let sit in the refrigerator for between 30 minutes and 4 hours. You can also soak the salmon for 2 hours in brine (see page 93) and add the pepper just before sautéing. Pat dry and season with pepper only if you've used brine just before sautéing.

Bring about 4 quarts of water to a rapid boil with a small handful of salt and toss in the spinach leaves. Push them down into the water with a wooden spoon and stir the around until they "melt," about 30 seconds. (Don't wait for the water to come back to the boil.) Drain in a colander, rinse with cold water, and gently squeeze the water from the spinach. Reserve.

Combine the shallots, garlic, and kaffir lime leaves in a small pot. Cut the hard root end off the lemon grass and peel off the outermost sheath from the stalk if it seems dry or hard. Starting from the root end, slice about 5 inches of the lemon grass as thinly as you can and add the slices to the pot. Add the optional galangal, the chopped chilies and 1 cup water. Bring to a simmer, cover the pot, and simmer gently for 10 minutes.

Remove the lid from the pot—stand back; the fumes from the chilies can reek havoc on the sinuses—and add the coconut milk and fish sauce. Bring to a simmer and add the lime juice and cilantro and simmer for 1 minute. If the broth needs salt, it usually needs more fish sauce, but if it tastes strong or overly fishy, add salt to taste instead.

Just before you're ready to serve, put the spinach in a saucepan with about a half cup of the Thai broth, cover the pot, and bring to a gentle simmer. Sauté the salmon fillets as described in the recipe on page 25.

Bring the remaining Thai broth to a simmer.

Arrange a small mound of spinach in the center of 6 heated soup plates. Place a salmon fillet on each mound—skin side up if the skin's attached, flesh side up if it isn't—and ladle the Thai broth around it. Serve immediately.

Handling Hot Chilies and Peppers: Seeding and chopping hot chilies will leave your fingers stinging and if you happen to rub your eyes, they will tear like crazy. Burning fingers never bother me, but if you have sensitive skin or are preparing a large quantity of hot chilies and peppers, wear surgical gloves when handling them.

A fresh poblano chili.

SALMON FILLETS WITH SHELLFISH
AND PARSLEY BROTH

Clams, cockles, or mussels can all be steamed open to provide a base for a savory broth you can use to surround sautéed, baked, poached, or grilled salmon fillets. Because the sauce should be made at the last minute, I sometimes bake the salmon fillets (see page 125) instead of sautéing them so I can fuss with the sauce while the salmon is cooking.

MAKES 4 MAIN-COURSE SERVINGS

> **four 6- to 8-ounce salmon fillets with the skin on or off**
> **salt**
> **pepper**
> **1 pound New Zealand cockles or mussels or 20 littleneck clams**
> **¾ cup dry white wine**
> **½ cup heavy cream**
> **2 tablespoons chopped parsley** (chopped at the last minute)
> **1 tablespoon olive oil**

Season the salmon fillets with salt and pepper and refrigerate until needed.

Rinse the cockles, mussels, or clams. If they're dirty scrub them with a stiff brush. Sort through and discard any dead ones. Clams should be firmly closed, cockles can gape a tiny bit but should close when you jostle them around. It's all right if mussels gape slightly, but they should close when you give them a good pinch.

Put the shellfish in a pot with the wine, cover, and bring to a simmer over medium heat. Cockles take about 4 minutes to open, mussels take about 6 minutes, and clams take closer to 12. Take the shellfish out of their shells— if you like, leave a few in the shell to look pretty in the plates—and slowly pour the cooking liquid into a wide sauté pan with a lid, leaving any grit behind in the pot. Add the cream, shellfish, and parsley to the steaming liquid and reserve.

Begin sautéing the salmon as described on page 25. (If you've doubled or tripled this recipe, you may want to bake it as described on page 125.)

While the salmon is cooking, cover the sauté pan and heat over medium to high heat while shaking it back and forth and gently stirring the shellfish with a wooden spoon. Don't let the mixture boil or you'll toughen the shellfish.

Arrange the salmon in heated soup plates and spoon the sauce and shellfish over and around. Serve immediately.

SAUTÉED SALMON WITH NOODLES AND VIETNAMESE SPICE BROTH

This is a simplified version of the Vietnamese national dish, pho, which contains varying proportions of liquids to solids and can range from what looks like a soup to a bowl of noodles with various condiments. In this version, adapted as a base for sautéed salmon, the emphasis is on the noodles so they can prop up the salmon and keep it from overcooking. In traditional recipes, *pho* is served with rice noodles, sometimes called rice vermicelli or rice sticks, which are sold in Asian groceries in little bunches that look like nests. Rice noodles should be soaked in cold water until they're soft and pliable, about 30 minutes, before they are cooked. If you don't want to bother seeking out rice noodles, use Japanese soba noodles or regular vermicelli noodles, following the directions on the package.

MAKES 6 MAIN-COURSE SERVINGS

> six 6- to 8-ounce salmon fillets with the skin on or off
> salt
> pepper
> 1½ tablespoon peanut oil or olive oil for sautéing the salmon

For the broth:
> 10 cups chicken broth
> 6 whole star anise
> two 2-inch lengths cinnamon stick
> 4 whole cloves
> two 2-inch pieces fresh ginger, each cut into about 8 slices
>   (don't bother peeling)
> 1 clove garlic, crushed and peeled
> 2 tablespoons sugar
> 1 medium onion, peeled and quartered
> 2 teaspoons black peppercorns
> 2 to 4 tablespoons Thai fish sauce or more to taste (optional)
> ¼ cup lemon juice

For the noodles:
> 1 pound (or two 6¾-ounce packages) rice noodles, soba noodles, or vermicelli

For the final garnish:
> leaves from 1 bunch cilantro, left whole
> leaves from 1 bunch mint, torn into small pieces just before adding

leaves from 1 bunch basil, preferably Thai basil or holy basil,
   (about 30), torn into small pieces
4 Thai or serrano chilies or 6 jalapeño chilies, stemmed, seeded,
   and chopped fine
4 tablespoons lime juice
3 scallions, including greens, sliced thin

Season the salmon with salt and pepper and refrigerate until needed.

If using rice noodles, soak for 30 minutes in cold water and drain in a colander.

Bring the chicken broth to a gentle simmer. Crush the star anise by placing it on a cutting board and rocking over it with the corner of a saucepan, using your weight to push down on the pan. Crush the cinnamon into splinters and the cloves in the same way. Add the anise, cinnamon, cloves, ginger, garlic, sugar, and onion to the simmering broth and simmer gently, covered, for 20 minutes. Just before you're ready to strain the broth, crush the peppercorns under a saucepan and stir them into the broth. Simmer for 1 minute. Stir in the fish sauce and taste the broth. If it seems to need more salt, add more fish sauce. Add the lemon juice and strain the broth through a fine-mesh strainer or a triple layer of cheesecloth and reserve.

About 10 minutes before you're ready to serve, bring 4 quarts of water to a boil.

Sauté the salmon fillets as described in the recipe on page 25. Bring the reserved broth to a gentle simmer while the salmon is sautéing.

Coordinate the noodle cooking with the salmon sautéing. If you're using rice noodles plunge them in the boiling salted water for about 30 seconds and immediately drain in a colander. If you're using soba noodles, cook them according to the directions on the package (usually for about 8 minutes—start them about the same time you start sautéing the salmon) but bite into a noodle every few minutes to know when they're done. If you're using vermicelli, follow the directions on the package.

When the salmon and noodles are just about ready, stir the cilantro, mint, basil, chilies, lime juice, and scallions into the simmering broth and simmer for 1 minute.

Use tongs to transfer mounds of noodles from the colander into heated deep bowls and ladle the broth over so it comes about halfway up the sides of the noodles. Place a piece of sautéed salmon (skin side up if you've left the skin on; flesh side up if you've removed the skin) on top of the noodles and serve.

GRILLING

Grilling fish terrifies a lot of us because some kinds of fish stick to the grill and fall apart when you turn them. Salmon—either steaks, fillets, or medallions—takes well to the grill because it has a relatively high fat content, which keeps it from sticking. It is also relatively firm-fleshed, which helps it hold together when you're turning it.

When you grill salmon, use a very hot grill so the salmon browns on the outside but is still moist and slightly translucent when you cut into it. (Don't confuse grilling with barbecue, which involves slow cooking and is actually more like smoking.) I like to use hardwood charcoal instead of briquets because it burns hotter and longer and has a more natural wood fragrance. It makes a marvelous crystalline sound when you're pouring it into the grill. But don't go crazy if you can't find it, briquets or even a gas grill will still produce delicious grilled salmon.

There are all sorts of ways to light your fire, including electric coils that almost always require long extension cords to reach out to the backyard, liquid starters with a kerosene smell that takes a long time to burn off, and, of course, old-fashioned kindling. The best method is to use a metal cylinder— sometimes called chimney—divided inside so that you can fill the top three quarters with charcoal and stuff the bottom quarter with newspaper. Amazingly, it works every time.

When grilling fish, it's especially important to make sure your grill is perfectly clean. I usually spray mine with heavy-duty oven cleaner (follow the precautions on the can), scrub it with steel wool, and rinse it thoroughly. When the coals are ready, let the grill rack heat for a few minutes and rub it quickly with a paper towel dipped in a little vegetable oil before putting on the salmon.

I like to grill salmon fillets with the skin on because I like its crispy, ever-so-slightly charred flavor and texture, but the skin tends to stick. There are several tricks for avoiding the sticking. The best method is to soak the salmon for 1 to 2 hours (depending on the salmon's thickness) in cold brine (see page 93) before grilling. Just before you put the salmon on the grill, make sure the salmon is perfectly dry—if you've seasoned it ahead of time the salt will have drawn out moisture—and then brush or rub it lightly with olive oil. If you're leaving the skin on, put the skin side down on the rack first. If you're grilling skinless fillets, put the flesh side down first. Turn the salmon over only once so there's less risk of it breaking apart. Many cooks make the mistake of sliding a spatula under fish fillets or steaks to turn them over, a tricky technique that makes it very easy to tear the surface of the fish and cause it to stick. It's better to slide a large, two-pronged fork under the salmon between the slats in the rack and gently detach the salmon from the rack before sliding under the spatula, holding the fork against the top of the salmon, and gently turning it over.

Even though grilling produces delicious results, grilled salmon tastes pretty much the same every time you grill it. You can change the flavor of grilled salmon by putting wet wood chips on the coals just before putting on the salmon, or you can add a small handful of wet herb sprigs, such as rosemary, thyme, or savory, so the smoke rises up and flavors the salmon. Both of these methods create rather subtle changes, but if you want more dramatic effects you can marinate the salmon with flavorful ingredients, coat it with chopped herbs, spices, or ground dried mushrooms, or brush it with a savory sauce during grilling. I like to serve grilled salmon with a variety of condiments—salsas, chutneys, sauces, and relishes—which guests can serve themselves.

Using a Grill Pan: There are times, regardless of weather, when I simply must have something grilled. I've grilled in snow and rain with friends holding umbrellas over me and the grill while suspicious neighbors peered warily out their windows. But lately such heroic efforts have become rare, especially since someone gave me a grill pan for my birthday. A grill pan is a heavy skillet with ridges. Other than rubbing the pan with a little oil, you don't use any cooking fat as you would when sautéing but simply place the pan over high heat on the stove until it becomes brutally hot. You then grill as you would on a regular grill. Two things to remember: keep the grill pan clean, which is almost impossible to do without using heavy-duty oven cleaner, and lift the salmon from the pan by sliding a two-pronged fork between the ridges in the pan under the fish instead of trying to use a spatula, which will tear the flesh or skin and cause sticking.

Serving the Best-Looking Side Up: Because one side of a salmon fillet is more attractive than the other, you should always start cooking the salmon with the most attractive side down so that when you turn the fillet over, the most attractive side is facing up on the plate. If you're grilling or sautéing salmon fillets with the skin on, start cooking with the skin side facing down so that the crispy (and attractive) skin faces up when you serve it. Salmon fillets that have had their skin removed have an unsightly coloration where the skin was. When cooking skin-off fillets, cook the skin side last so the more attractive side of the salmon—the side that was facing the backbone—ends facing up on the plate.

Crosshatch Grill Marks: I'm always irritated by those pictures in hotel elevators showing pieces of grilled meat or fish with a perfect crosshatch pattern lightly charred into the surface. I've been on enough photo shoots to know that those markings are burned in with a hot iron rod. But I have to admit that that square grid is attractive. To pull it off, you need a grill with a rack made of heavy iron instead of he more typical thick wire found on most home barbecues. Second, you need to give the first side of whatever it is you're grilling a 90 degree turn halfway through the grilling of that side.

BASIC GRILLED SALMON

> **six 6- to 8-ounce salmon fillets with the skin on or off, steaks, or medallions**
> (see page 20)
> **salt** (or ½ recipe brine, see page 93)
> **pepper**
> **1 tablespoon olive oil**

Season the salmon liberally on both sides with salt and pepper and let sit in the refrigerator for between 30 minutes and 4 hours, or soak it in cold brine for 2 hours. If you're brining the salmon, be sure the brine covers it—I usually weight the salmon down with a plate. Just before grilling, pat the salmon dry. If you've used brine, season it only with pepper.

Build a charcoal fire or fire up the gas grill with the grill about 6 inches from the heat source. (Some grills aren't adjustable so you'll have to mound up the coals; if you're using a gas grill, set it on high and turn it down to medium about 5 minutes before putting on the salmon.) Rub or brush the salmon on both sides with olive oil and rub the grill with a paper towel with a tiny bit of oil on it. Place skin-on salmon fillets skin side down on the grill, or skin-off salmon fillets flesh side down on the grill and grill for 3 to 4 minutes for 1-inch thick salmon. Turn the salmon over with a fork and spatula and grill for 3 to 4 minutes on the second side. Test if it's done by feeling it with your finger to see if it's firm, or by cutting into a piece. Gently transfer to a hot plate.

MISO-MARINATED GRILLED SALMON

Most of us have tasted miso soup in Japanese restaurants—I never tire of it—but few of us make it ourselves. Miso is a salty paste made from fermented soy beans; it is far more aromatic and delicately flavored than most soy sauce. It makes a perfect marinade and glaze for grilled foods including, of course, salmon. Miso comes in various colors, ranging from very pale brown, almost beige, to deep reddish brown. In general, paler miso paste is more mild and less salty. When given a choice, I opt for a medium brown.

MAKES 6 MAIN-COURSE SERVINGS

3 tablespoons brown miso paste

3 tablespoons white wine or sake

6 tablespoons mirin, or 2 tablespoons sugar dissolved in 4 tablespoons boiling water

six 6- to 8-ounce salmon fillets, skin and pin bones removed

2 tablespoons peanut or olive oil

Whisk together the miso, white wine, and mirin in a mixing bowl large enough to hold the salmon. Put the salmon in the bowl, rub it all over with the miso paste, and let it marinate in the refrigerator for 4 to 6 hours. Just before grilling, wipe the marinade off the salmon and rub the salmon with a tablespoon of the oil.

Fire up the grill, rub the grill just before grilling with a paper towel dipped in the remaining oil, and grill the salmon fillets until done, 3 to 4 minutes on each side.

Serve miso-marinated salmon fillets with rice and a cool cucumber salad or one of the salsas on page 69–72.

GRILLED SALMON WITH HOISIN
AND SESAME GLAZE

I've always found Chinese dishes made with hoisin sauce to be cloyingly sweet, but hoisin sauce, combined with some sesame oil and garlic, makes a perfect accent to the rich full flavor of grilled or hot-smoked salmon. In this dish I sprinkle the salmon with toasted sesame seeds for added flavor.

MAKES 6 MAIN-COURSE SERVINGS

> **six 6- to 8-ounce salmon fillets, skin and pin bones removed**
> **salt** (or ½ recipe brine, see page 93)
> **pepper**
> **¼ cup hoisin sauce**
> **1 clove garlic,** chopped fine and crushed to a paste with
>   the side of a chefs' knife
> **2 teaspoons dark Asian sesame oil** (preferably a Japanese brand)
> **1 tablespoon sherry vinegar or white wine vinegar**
> **2 tablespoons peanut or olive oil**
> **3 tablespoons white or black sesame seeds, or a combination** (optional)

Season the salmon liberally on both sides with salt and pepper and let sit in the refrigerator for between 30 minutes and 4 hours, or soak it in brine in the refrigerator for 2 hours. Place a plate on top of the salmon to keep it submerged. Pat the salmon dry just before grilling. If you've used brine, season it only with pepper.

Combine the hoisin sauce, garlic, sesame oil, and vinegar and smear 2 table-spoons of this mixture over the salmon. Refrigerate, covered, for 4 to 8 hours. Reserve the rest of the hoisin mixture. Just before grilling, wipe off the hoisin mixture with a paper towel and rub the salmon with a tablespoon of the oil.

Stir the sesame seeds in a heavy-bottomed pan (I use an iron skillet) over medium heat for about 5 minutes until they smell fragrant. If you're using white sesame seeds, they should lightly brown. Reserve.

Fire up the grill, rub the grill just before grilling with a paper towel dipped in the remaining oil, and grill the salmon, remembering to put the flesh side down on the grill first for 3 to 4 minutes. Turn the salmon over and spoon the remaining hoisin sauce mixture over it. Continue brushing or spooning the mixture over the salmon while it is grilling until you've used all the mixture, cooking for 3 to 4 minutes. Sprinkle with the optional sesame seeds and serve on heated plates.

GRILLED SALMON WITH KETCHUP AND TARRAGON GLAZE

Ketchup, long relegated to hamburgers and French fries, has suddenly become popular in some of the world's most expensive restaurants. It's easy to use as a glaze for any number of grilled foods, salmon being no exception. I liven it up with fresh tarragon, but other fresh herbs, such as basil, marjoram, thyme, and savory, each add their own special effects to the basic glaze.

MAKES 6 MAIN-COURSE SERVINGS

six 6- to 8-ounce salmon fillets, skin on or off, pin bones removed
salt (or ½ recipe brine, see page 93)
pepper
6 tablespoons ketchup
2 tablespoons balsamic vineger
3 tablespoons fresh tarragon leaves (leaves from 1 medium bunch)
2 tablespoons olive oil
oil for the grill

Season the salmon liberally on both sides with salt and pepper and let sit in the refrigerator for between 30 minutes and 4 hours, or soak it in brine in the refrigerator for 2 hours. Place a plate on top of the salmon to keep it submerged. Pat the salmon dry just before grilling. If you've used brine, season it only with pepper.

Combine the ketchup and vinegar in a small mixing bowl. Sprinkle the tarragon leaves with a teaspoon of the oil on a cutting board. The oil keeps tarragon and basil from turning black. Chop the tarragon and stir it into the ketchup mixture.

Rub the salmon fillets on both sides with 2 tablespoons of the ketchup mixture and refrigerate for 4 to 8 hours. Just before grilling, rub the marinade off the salmon with a paper towel and rub the salmon with a tablespoon of the oil.

Fire up the grill, rub the grill just before grilling with a paper towel dipped in the remaining oil, and grill the salmon, skin side down first if you're leaving the skin on and the flesh side down first if you're using skinless fillets. Grill for 3 to 4 minutes, then turn the salmon over and brush or spoon the ketchup glaze over it. Continue brushing or spooning on the glaze while the salmon is grilling for 3 to 4 minutes more, until you've used all the mixture. Serve on heated plates.

GRILLED SALMON WITH CORN, TOMATO, AND CHILI BROTH

This spicy soup is delicious by itself but makes an even better accent to grilled salmon.

MAKES 6 MAIN-COURSE SERVINGS

> **six 6- to 8-ounce salmon fillets, skin on or off, steaks, or medallions** (see page 20)
>
> **salt**
>
> **pepper**
>
> **1 tablespoon olive oil**
>
> **4 ears corn,** shucked
>
> **1 cup chicken broth**
>
> **2 ripe tomatoes,** peeled, seeded, and chopped
>
> **2 jalapeño chilies,** seeded and chopped fine
>
> **2 dried chipotle chilies** (soaked for 1 hour in warm water) or chipotle chilies in adobo sauce, seeded and chopped
>
> **1 teaspoon fresh thyme leaves or ½ teaspoon dried thyme,** chopped fine
>
> **leaves from 1 medium bunch cilantro,** chopped at the last minute
>
> **2 cups sour cream**

Season the salmon pieces with salt and pepper, rub them with olive oil, and reserve in the refrigerator for 30 minutes to 4 hours.

Scrape the kernels off the corn cobs by holding each ear in a large bowl and scraping down along the ear with a sharp paring knife. You should have about 3 cups. Combine the corn with the chicken broth in a blender and puree for 1 minute. Push the mixture through a strainer with the back of a ladle or put through a food mill. Stir the tomatoes, chilies, thyme, and cilantro into the corn soup. Season to taste with salt and pepper and reserve. Just before you grill the salmon, bring it to a gentle simmer.

Grill the salmon for 3 to 4 minutes on each side. Place servings in the center of heated soup plates. Spoon the corn soup around and dollop each serving with sour cream. Pass the rest of the sour cream at the table.

Variation: For dramatic effect, and to make this dish a complete meal, I sometimes place a mound of cooked spinach or sorrel in the center of each soup plate to prop up the salmon.

Salsas, Sauces, and Condiments for Grilled Salmon

While there are special ways of preparing salmon for the grill, such as rubbing it with spice or herb mixtures, brining or curing it, or marinating in a flavorful liquid, the most dramatic effects are often produced in the easiest ways—by serving plain grilled salmon with one or more homemade condiments. It's hard to define a condiment exactly, but I usually think of it as some ingredient that guests pass at the table and serve themselves.

There are many different kinds of condiments which range from hollandaise sauce (a condiment since it's traditionally served on the side), to various homemade French mayonnaises, to Mexican salsa-like condiments that may contain chiles, tomatoes, avocados, or corn. There are chutneys, which usually contain sweet and sour ingredients and often fruits, and there are relishes made by chopping together pickled ingredients such as cucumbers. One of my favorite condiments started out as a tropical fruit salad but turned into a magnificent condiment when I added some chilies and chopped the fruits into smaller pieces.

Opposite, clockwise from top: *Dried Wild Mushroom Mayonnaise (page 67), Tarragon Butter (page 114), Tropical Fruit Salsa (page 71), Yogurt and Cucumber Salsa (page 69), and Chili Mayonnaise (page 66).*

BASIC MAYONNAISE MADE IN A BLENDER OR FOOD PROCESSOR

The idea of putting mayonnaise on grilled anything sounds revolting to anybody who associates mayonnaise with the stiff white kind found in a jar. Mayonnaise that you make yourself with fresh eggs and good-quality oil offers an entirely different experience and the mayonnaise itself is easy to convert into an amazing number of tasty sauces. I sometimes make a big batch of basic mayonnaise with just egg yolks, mustard, a little vinegar, and vegetable oil, and then flavor it with different ingredients. Added ingredients also lighten the mayonnaise and make it less rich. I then pass the different mayonnaises around the table for guests to dollop on their grilled salmon.

If you want to make mayonnaise by hand, see the recipe for garlic mayonnaise (aïoli) on page 43.

MAKES 2 CUPS (ENOUGH FOR ABOUT 8 MAIN-COURSE
SERVINGS OF GRILLED SALMON)

3 egg yolks (see box on page 68 if you're worried about eating
  raw egg yolks)
1 teaspoon salt
2 tablespoons Dijon-style mustard
2 tablespoons good-quality white wine vinegar
1½ cups canola or other vegetable oil with no distinct taste or aroma

Combine the egg yolks, salt, mustard, and vinegar in a blender or food processor. If you're using a blender, start at slow speed. With the blender or food processor running, pour the oil slowly—in a very thin, steady stream—through the opening at the top of the lid. When you see the mayonnaise starting to stiffen, you can add the oil a little faster. When the mayonnaise gets so stiff that it no longer moves around in the blender, add up to 4 tablespoons of water, a tablespoon at a time, until it moves around again. Transfer the mayonnaise to a bowl with a rubber spatula.

Chili Mayonnaise (see page 66).

CHILI MAYONNAISE

This mayonnaise is quite hot, but if you want it milder, increase the amount of bell pepper and decrease the amounts of poblanos and chipotles. Chipotle chilies, which are smoked jalapeño chilies, are available dried or canned, usually in a kind of tomato sauce called adobo sauce. Don't feel limited to using chipotle and poblano chilies, although they are easier to find than other, more exotic chilies. The chipotle chilies add a delightful complex smoky flavor.

MAKES 1½ TO 2 CUPS

1 or 2 dried chipotle chilies or chipotle chilies in adobo sauce
1 red bell pepper
1 fresh poblano chili (optional)
2 tablespoons chopped cilantro
1 cup basic mayonnaise (see page 65)
salt

If you're using dried chipotle chilies, rinse them under cold water to eliminate dust and then soak them in just enough warm water to cover until they're soft and pliable, about 40 minutes. If you're using chilies in adobo sauce, just take one or two out of the can (you can freeze the rest in a plastic container) and rinse off the sauce. Stem, seed, and chop the chilies. You may want to wear gloves—otherwise your fingers will sting.

Roast, peel and seed the bell pepper and poblano chili according to the directions on page 77. Chop the peppers fine. Stir the chopped peppers and cilantro into the mayonnaise and, if needed, season to taste with salt.

DRIED WILD MUSHROOM
MAYONNAISE

Because dried wild porcini mushrooms and dried morels have a more pronounced flavor than fresh, they become highly addictive when combined with a basic mayonnaise.

MAKES 1½ CUPS

> **1 cup dried morel or porcini mushrooms, or a combination**
> **¾ cup basic mayonnaise** (see page 65)
> **salt**
> **pepper**

Rinse the mushrooms under cold running water to eliminate dust. Put them in a bowl with ¼ cup cold water and soak for about 30 minutes, until they're soft and pliable. Stir them around in the water every 10 minutes so they soak evenly. Squeeze them firmly in your hand—hold them over the bowl to capture any of the soaking liquid—and chop them to the consistency of hamburger relish. Stir the chopped mushrooms into the mayonnaise. If the mayonnaise is very stiff, gently pour in some of the soaking liquid, leaving any grit behind, until it has the consistency you like. Season to taste with salt and pepper. Let sit at least 1 hour at room temperature before serving, to release the flavor of the mushrooms.

HERB AND CAPER MAYONNAISE

This is a derivative of a classic tartar sauce, but it contains a lot more capers and herbs so it is less rich and has a brighter, tangier flavor. If you don't have all the herbs, just substitute more of the others. This sauce is also good made with fresh basil.

MAKES 1¾ CUPS

> **2 heaping tablespoons capers,** drained and chopped
>
> **8 cornichons (French-style sour gherkins),** chopped to the consistency of hamburger relish
>
> **2 tablespoons finely chopped fresh chives**
>
> **2 tablespoons finely chopped fresh tarragon** (rub the leaves with a teaspoon of olive oil and chop them at the last minute or they will turn black)
>
> **2 tablespoons finely chopped fresh parsley**
>
> **1 cup basic mayonnaise** (see page 65)
>
> **salt**

Combine the capers, cornichons, chives, tarragon, parsley, and mayonnaise and season to taste with salt, which you may not need because the gherkins and capers are salty.

What About Raw Egg Yolks? Even though nowadays the chances of encountering a contaminated egg are very small, you may not want to take the chance. This is especially true if you're making a very large batch of mayonnaise, in which case the chances of including a contaminated yolk increase. To avoid the risk, combine a tablespoon of water with each egg yolk in a metal mixing bowl or a saucepan with sloping sides, sometimes called a Windsor pan. Put the pan or bowl over medium heat (if you're using a bowl, hold its edge with an oven mitt) and whisk the yolks until they froth and the mixture then stiffens so that you see the bottom of the bowl while you're whisking. Immediately take the yolks off the heat and whisk for a minute more, so they don't overcook and scramble. Beat or blend in the oil as you would when making the basic mayonnaise on page 65.

YOGURT AND CUCUMBER SALSA

Cucumber salads show up in Mediterranean countries, in the Middle East, and in India. In France we used to make one with mint and crème fraîche; in Iran they add walnuts and raisins. But it was an Indian *raita* of cucumbers in yogurt—served as a cool and refreshing side dish to accompany fiery curries—that gave me the idea of converting it into a salsa to dollop on grilled fish. It's especially good on salmon because its lightness and tang contrast with the salmon's rich, deep flavors.

MAKES 2 CUPS (ENOUGH FOR 4 MAIN-COURSE SERVINGS)

1 cup plain whole milk yogurt

2 long hot house cucumbers, or 3 regular cucumbers, peeled

1 tablespoon coarse sea salt or kosher salt

1 small red onion, finely chopped, or **3 scallions,**
  whites and half the greens sliced thin

2 tablespoons finely chopped mint

2 tablespoons finely chopped cilantro

1 tablespoon lemon juice

pepper

Put the yogurt in a strainer lined with a coffee filter or a sheet of muslin (well-rinsed to eliminate any traces of soap), or a triple layer of cheesecloth. Set the strainer over a bowl and let drain for 3 to 6 hours in the refrigerator.

Cut the cucumbers in half lengthwise and scoop out the seeds with a spoon. Cut each half into ¼-inch thick strips and then into ¼-inch cubes. Rub the cucumber cubes with the coarse salt—keep rubbing until all the salt has dissolved and you don't feel it on your fingers—and let drain in a colander for 30 minutes.

Squeeze the water out of the cucumbers a small handful at a time. Toss the cucumbers with onion, mint, cilantro, lemon juice, and drained yogurt. Season with pepper and refrigerate for at least 30 minutes before serving.

TROPICAL FRUIT SALSA

In Italy and Mexico, salsa means sauce, but in America "salsa" has come to mean a mixture of chopped raw or mostly raw ingredients, usually dolloped on foods (or eaten with chips) as a condiment. The most popular salsas contain chopped tomatoes, but salsas often include avocados, chilies, corn, onions, garlic, and various herbs and spices. This one features tropical fruits enlivened with chilies and grilled bell peppers.

MAKES 4 CUPS (ENOUGH FOR 8 MAIN-COURSE SERVINGS)

2 dried chipotle chilies or chipotle chilies in adobo sauce, or 3 jalapeño chilies
¼ **small pineapple,** peeled, cored, and cut into wedges
1 Hawaiian papaya, peeled, seeded, and cut into chunks
2 kiwis, peeled and sliced
1 ripe mango, halved, pit removed and fruit cut from skin
1 medium red onion, chopped fine
1 red bell pepper, charred, skinned, stemmed, seeded, and chopped (see page 77)
juice from 2 limes
leaves from 1 medium bunch cilantro, chopped fine
salt

If you're using dried chipotle chilies, rinse them under cold water to eliminate dust and then soak them in just enough warm water to cover until they're soft and pliable, about 40 minutes. If you're using chilies in adobo sauce, rinse off the sauce. If you're using jalapeño chilies, leave them raw. Stem, seed, and chop all the chilies. You may want to wear gloves—otherwise your fingers will sting.

Combine the pineapple, papaya, kiwis, and mango in a food processor and pulse them to a chunky semi-liquid consistency, but don't overdo it or you'll turn the salsa into soup. If you don't have a food processor, chop the fruits by hand.

Combine the chopped fruit mixture with the chilies, onion, bell pepper, lime juice, and cilantro in a mixing bowl. Cover with plastic wrap and chill in the refrigerator for at least 2 hours. Pass at the table to dollop on grilled or sautéed salmon.

TOMATO AND AVOCADO SALSA

This cool and spicy salsa is similar to a guacamole, but the vegetables are chopped instead of crushed. You can make this salsa in a food processor, but you'll get a much nicer effect if you chop the ingredients by hand.

MAKES 2 CUPS (ENOUGH FOR 4 MAIN-COURSE SERVINGS)

> **2 dried chipotle chilies or chipotle chilies in adobo sauce, or 3 jalapeño chilies**
> **3 ripe medium tomatoes**
> **1 clove garlic,** chopped fine
> **1 red bell pepper,** seeds removed and chopped fine
> **1 jalapeño chili,** seeded and chopped fine
> **1 poblano chili,** charred, peeled, seeded, and chopped fine (see page 77)
> **1 medium red onion,** chopped fine
> **1 avocado, preferably Hass,** peeled and chopped at the last minute
> **leaves from 1 large bunch of cilantro**
> **¼ cup lime juice** (juice of 1 or 2 limes)
> **salt**

If you're using dried chipotle chilies, rinse them under cold water to eliminate dust and then soak them in just enough warm water to cover until they're soft and pliable, about 40 minutes. If you're using chilies in adobo sauce, rinse off the sauce. Stem, seed, and chop the chilies. You may want to wear gloves—otherwise your fingers will sting.

Cut the stems from the tomatoes and peel them by submerging them in a pot of boiling water for about 30 seconds, quickly rinsing them in cold water, and pulling the peel away with your fingers or a paring knife. Seed them by cutting them in half crosswise and squeezing the seeds out of each half. Chop the tomatoes to a medium consistency.

Combine chilies, tomatoes, garlic, bell pepper, onion, avocado, cilantro, and lime juice, season to taste with salt, and let mixture sit for an hour or two in the refrigerator before serving.

GRILLED SALMON SALAD NIÇOISE

When summer rolls around, most of my cooking is done outdoors on the grill so I don't have to turn on the oven or stove and heat up the house. A favorite formula is to grill steak, tuna, or salmon and then combine the grilled meat or fish with fresh salad greens, tomatoes, sometimes hard-boiled eggs, homemade croutons, string beans (ideally the thin French kind), pitted olives and, unless my guests object, anchovies. With firm-fleshed foods like steak or tuna, I combine all the ingredients in a big bowl and toss them together at the table, but when I use salmon, I arrange the salad ingredients individually on each plate because salmon is too fragile to toss. Below is one of my more elaborate versions. Feel free to leave out any of the ingredients and use more of the others.

MAKES 6 MAIN-COURSE SERVINGS

six 6-ounce salmon fillets with the skin on or off, grilled (see page 57)
   or **sautéed** (see page 25) or **hot-smoked salmon** (see page 98)

salt

pepper

3 medium waxy potatoes, about 1 pound total

6 tablespoons good-quality vinegar

¾ cup extra-virgin olive oil

4 ripe tomatoes

1 pound green beans, preferably thin French *haricots verts*, ends broken off

6 handfuls mixed greens, such as arugula, basil leaves, baby oak leaf
   lettuce, baby radicchio, or mesclun mix, washed and dried

⅔ cup pitted brine-cured black olives (don't use canned olives)

3 hard-boiled eggs, peeled and cut into 4 wedges each

6 thin slices smoked salmon (about ¼ pound), cut into 2-inch-wide strips
   (optional)

2 red bell peppers, peeled, stemmed, seeded, and cut into ¼-inch wide strips
   (see page 77)

18 anchovy fillets, patted dry on paper towels (optional)

Season the salmon on both sides with salt and pepper and refrigerate until needed.

Put the potatoes in a pot with just enough cold water to cover and bring to a gentle simmer. When the potatoes are easily penetrated with a knife, after about 30 minutes, drain the potatoes and pull away the peels with a paring knife while holding the hot potato in a towel. Cut the potatoes into ½-inch thick slices and spread them on a platter or in a large bowl. Season them with salt and pepper, sprinkle them with 1 tablespoon vinegar and 2 tablespoons extra virgin olive oil, and reserve.

If you're peeling the tomatoes, bring about 4 quarts of water to a boil. Wash the tomatoes and dip them in the boiling water for about 30 seconds, immediately transfer them to a colander with a slotted spoon, and rinse with cold water. (Keep the water on the stove for the beans.) Cut out the stem end and pull away the peel with your fingers or a small paring knife. Cut the tomatoes into about 6 wedges each, depending on their size, and push the seeds out of the sides of the wedges with your forefinger. Reserve in a large salad bowl.

Toss a handful of salt in the water you used for the tomatoes, bring it back to a rolling boil, and add the green beans. Cook them until they lose their crunch but not until they turn mushy, about 6 minutes. (The only way to know when they're done is to take one out and bite into it.) Drain in a colander and rinse immediately with cold water. After draining for 5 minutes, spin the beans completely dry in a salad spinner and put them in the bowl with the tomatoes.

Grill or sauté the salmon and combine the potatoes, tomatoes, beans, greens, and olives in the bowl. Dress with the remaining oil and vinegar. Gently toss the salad—the best and gentlest way is to use your fingers—until all the ingredients are well combined. Arrange the salad on 6 plates. Leave a space with just greens in the middle of each plate. When the salmon is ready, place 1 fillet in the center of each salad. Arrange the egg wedges, strips of smoked salmon, peppers, and anchovies over and around the salmon. Serve immediately.

Peeling Bell Peppers and Chilies

Gas Stove Method: Arrange the peppers or chilies right over the burners with the flame turned on high. Turn them over every couple of minutes until they are thoroughly charred and coated with black. If any section of the pepper becomes coated with white ash, you're overdoing it—move that part of the pepper out of the flame.

Electric Stove Method: Make a rack for the peppers or chilies by bending down each end of a wire coat hanger and resting it on the electric stove coils. The wire should keep the chilies about an ⅛ of an inch above the red hot coils. Turn the heat up to high and roast the chilies, turning them every few minutes with tongs, until they are covered with black charred skin. If any part of the chilies starts to turn white, that part is overcooking.

Grill Method: I rarely build a charcoal fire just for grilling peppers or chilies but if you're barbecuing anyway, just grill the peppers or chilies—turning them from time to time with tongs—until they are blackened on all sides.

Broiler Method: Arrange the peppers or chilies so they're about ½ inch from the broiler flames. Rotate every minute or so with tongs so they blacken evenly. Watch the peppers carefully—some broilers will blacken them very quickly.

Peeling and Seeding the Peppers or Chilies: Put the charred peppers in a plastic bag for 10 minutes and pull off the charred peel with your fingers. Scrape off any stubborn patches of peel with a paring knife. Quickly rinse the chilies under cold running water to eliminate any flecks of peel. Pat dry with paper towels. Cut out the stems with a paring knife and cut the peppers lengthwise in half. Spoon out the seeds and pull out any large pieces of white pulp.

SALMON AND CHICORY SALAD

Chicory and bacon salad is one of my standby first courses in French restaurants. The hot smoky bacon makes a savory counterpoint to the bitter greens. It's easy to convert this classic salad into a main course or luxurious first course by adding other ingredients. Of course this applies to salmon, ideally just grilled or hot smoked, but it's also good with cooked salmon left over from the night before.

MAKES 6 FIRST-COURSE OR LIGHT MAIN-COURSE SERVINGS

4 large handfuls chicory (sometimes called curly endive, *frisée,* or *ricchia*), about two 10-ounce bunches

six ⅓-inch thick lean bacon slices (about 14 ounces total), or the equivalent weight of thinner slices, cut crosswise into 1-inch long strips

6 slices dense-crumb good-quality white bread, crusts removed and cut into ½-inch cubes

6 tablespoons good-quality wine vinegar, or more as needed

¾ cup extra-virgin olive oil

four 4- to 6-ounce salmon fillets with the skin on or off, sautéed (see page 25), **grilled** (see page 57), **hot-smoked** (see page 98), or left over

salt

pepper

6 slices smoked salmon, cut into 2-inch wide strips (optional)

Wash and dry the chicory and put it in a large salad bowl.

Heat the bacon strips in a heavy-bottomed skillet over medium heat, stirring every few minutes, until they just turn evenly crisp. Scoop out the bacon with a slotted spoon and reserve. Add the bread cubes and toss them in the bacon fat over medium heat until they are evenly browned and crisp and reserve in a bowl.

Prepare the salmon fillets. If you've sautéed the salmon, wipe the fat out of the pan and pour in the vinegar and olive oil. If you haven't sautéed the salmon, put the vinegar and oil in the pan used for cooking the bacon and croutons and bring to a simmer. Put the bacon in the vinegar-oil mixture to reheat it, grind some pepper over it, and pour everything over the greens.

Toss the salad and arrange it on individual plates. Place a piece of salmon in the center of each salad, sprinkle the croutons over it, and if you're using the smoked salmon, arrange the strips on the greens around the salmon.

Serve immediately.

SALMON "TANDOORI"

Since it's virtually impossible to make authentic tandoori at home (you need a special, very hot clay oven) I can't say this recipe is entirely authentic, but it's close. The marinade of garlic, ginger, cumin, yogurt, and cardamom is traditional. Instead of using a clay oven, I thread thick chunks of salmon on skewers and arrange them over a bed of hot coals. If you have a small hibachi–style grill you can arrange metal skewers across the grill without even using the rack. In this way the salmon cubes are suspended over the coals instead of touching the rack, which can cause sticking unless the marinade is completely wiped off and the cubes tossed in oil before being slid on skewers. If your grill is large or your skewers too small to span from one side to the other, just grill directly on the rack as described below. Unless you have skewers that have a thin, flat surface and aren't round, use two skewers per kebab so you can rotate the salmon without it swiveling. If you're grilling the skewers directly on the rack, you'll need to start this recipe the day before serving. This recipe is inspired by a chicken tandoori recipe in Julie Sahni's excellent book, *Classic Indian Cooking*.

MAKES 8 FIRST-COURSE OR 4 MAIN-COURSE SERVINGS

1½ to 2 pounds salmon fillet, without the skin and pin bones removed, cut from a section that is 1 to 1½ inches thick

½ recipe brine (see page 93)

12 whole green cardamom pods

4 teaspoons ground cumin

2 tablespoons ground coriander seeds

3 cloves garlic, chopped fine and crushed to a paste with the side of a chefs' knife

2-inch section ginger root, peeled and grated fine (about 4 tablespoons)

4 Thai or serrano chilies or 8 jalapeño chilies, stemmed, halved, seeding optional (the mixture will be hotter with the seeds left in), and chopped fine

½ cup plain whole milk yogurt

leaves from 1 medium bunch cilantro, chopped coarse just before you use them

3 tablespoons peanut oil (if you're grilling the salmon cubes directly on the rack)

Cut the salmon into 1-to-1½-inch cubes. Be sure to end up with a number divisible by 4 so every skewer gets the same number of cubes. Soak the cubes in the brine in the refrigerator for 2 hours.

Crush the cardamom pods by leaning on them with a heavy saucepan. Pick out the tiny black seeds with your fingers, crush them with the pan, and chop them with a chefs' knife.

Combine the cardamon, cumin, coriander, garlic, ginger, chilies, yogurt, and cilantro in a mixing bowl. Remove the salmon from the brine and combine it with the marinade using your hands. Cover the bowl with plastic wrap and refrigerate. Marinate the cubes for 12 to 24 hours.

Fire up the grill. Rinse the marinade from the salmon cubes, pat them dry, and toss them in a bowl with the peanut oil. Thread the salmon on skewers—if you're using wooden skewers, make sure the cubes touch each other—and wrap the ends of the skewers in aluminum foil. Grill the skewered salmon for about 2 minutes on each side with the grill rack 4 to 6 inches above the coals.

Place 1 or 2 skewers on hot plates and serve immediately.

FRESH VIETNAMESE-STYLE SALMON SPRING ROLLS

Vietnamese cooks make two kinds of spring rolls—fresh, in which the ingredients are cooked ahead of time and the spring roll served cold, and fried. In Vietnam, spring rolls usually contain shrimp and pork, but the technique works marvelously well with salmon.

Spring rolls require rice paper, which is completely edible and is sold, usually in three sizes, in thin translucent rounds. It's easy to find in Asian markets but you can also order it (see sources, page 156). Rice paper is dipped, a sheet or two at a time, in warm water, which turns it from crisp to pliable in a matter of seconds. Many spring rolls contain rice vermicelli noodles, but you can get by without them.

These fresh spring rolls make marvelous hors d'oeuvres, first courses, or side dishes if you're serving an assortment of Asian dishes at the same time.

MAKES 12 ROLLS (6 HORS-D'OEUVRE OR SIDE-DISH SERVINGS OR 4 FIRST-COURSE SERVINGS)

1 pound salmon fillet with the skin and pin bones removed
salt
pepper
1½ tablespoons peanut or olive oil
¼ pound rice vermicelli noodles or regular Italian dried vermicelli noodles
1 tablespoon salt (if you're using Italian noodles)
1 tablespoon olive oil (if you're using Italian noodles)
6 thin slices smoked salmon, about 6 inches square (optional)
twelve 8 ½-inch rounds rice paper
12 small crisp lettuce leaves, rinsed and dried (if you have large leaves, cut them in half along the rib)
¼ cup dry-roasted peanuts, coarsely chopped by hand or pulsed in a food processor
1 medium onion, preferably red, halved through the root end and sliced thin
1 clove garlic, chopped fine
1 cup bean sprouts
leaves from 1 medium bunch cilantro
leaves from 1 small bunch mint, torn into several pieces each
    (do this at the last minute or they'll turn black and lose flavor)

For the dipping sauce:

¼ cup Vietnamese or Thai fish sauce (see sources, page 156)
¼ cup rice vinegar (make sure the bottle doesn't say "rice flavored vinegar";

Kikkoman is my favorite brand)
- **3 tablespoons lime juice** (from 1 lime)
- **1 tablespoon sugar**
- **1 Thai chile or 2 jalapeño chilies,** stemmed, seeded, and chopped fine
- **1 clove garlic,** chopped fine and crushed to a paste with the side of a chefs' knife

Season the salmon on both sides with salt and pepper and refrigerate for at least 30 minutes but as long as 12 hours. Pat the salmon dry with paper towels and sauté in the peanut oil over high heat in a heavy-bottomed, preferably nonstick, pan. Sauté for about 4 minutes on each side per inch of thickness. Transfer to a plate covered with a triple layer of paper towels—to absorb burned fat—and pat the fillets on top with paper towels. Put in the refrigerator to cool.

Soak the rice noodles in cold water for 20 minutes and drain in a colander. If you're using Italian noodles, follow directions; drain and rinse. Toss with the olive oil to prevent sticking.

Cut the salmon fillet into 12 finger-shaped strips about 3 inches long. Cut the slices of smoked salmon in half and gently wrap around the salmon strips.

Fill a medium bowl with barely warm water. Dip rice paper into the water for about 10 seconds (don't try to work with more than two at a time or they'll tear) and arrange them on the work surface. Place a lettuce leaf over the bottom half of each round, sprinkle a few chopped peanuts, some onion slices, a tiny bit of garlic, and a pinch of bean sprouts over the bottom third of each round. Leave 1½ inches on each side bare, except the lettuce leaves. Arrange a salmon strip horizontally in the middle, and sprinkle some cilantro and mint leaves and tiny mound of noodles over it. Remember to use only $\frac{1}{12}$ of ingredients per spring roll. Start to roll the spring roll into a cylinder. As soon as the part facing you wraps under the filling, fold in the sides. Roll into a finished cylinder.

Put the spring rolls on a plate and cover them with a moist towel so they don't dry out. They can be kept in this way for up to 3 hours before serving.

To prepare the dipping sauce, stir together the fish sauce, vinegar, lime juice, sugar, chilies, and garlic until the sugar dissolves. It will keep in the refrigerator.

Pass the spring rolls as an hors d'oeuvre with the dipping sauce in a small dish on the platter, or serve 3 per person, on plates, as a first course. The spring rolls can be cut in half on a diagonal to create a decorative effect, as shown in the photo at left.

SALMON SAMOSAS

Anyone who has been to an Indian restaurant has probably encountered samosas, crisp, stuffed fried triangles served with one or more dipping sauces as an hors d'oeuvre.

If you want to make samosas with homemade dough, I highly recommend Julie Sahni's book, *Classic Indian Cooking*. I cheat and use round wonton wrappers, which is utterly heretical and limits you to making miniature samosas, but I use a filling that is Indian in spirit. In India most samosas are filled with ground meat or potatoes. Here, salmon is combined with curry, apples, cilantro, ginger, chilies, and garlic. To grate the ginger, use a paring knife to cut away the peel over about a 1-inch section and then grate it with a fine mesh grater. These samosas are also an excellent way to use salmon trimmings left over from another dish. If you want to make samosas ahead of time, you can refrigerate them on sheet pans for a day or you can freeze them on an oiled sheet pan and, once frozen, put them in plastic bags and back in the freezer. They need to be frozen before you put them into the bags or they'll stick to each other.

MAKES ABOUT 80

1 pound salmon fillets with the skin and pin bones removed,
   cut into 1-inch cubes
salt
pepper
5¼ cups peanut oil
2 medium red onions, chopped fine
4 Golden Delicious or other apples, peeled, cored, and chopped coarse
6 jalapeño peppers, stemmed, seeded, and chopped fine
3 garlic cloves, chopped fine
¼ cup grated fresh ginger
3 tablespoons good-quality curry powder
leaves from one medium bunch cilantro, chopped coarse
   (chopped just before you're ready to incorporate them into the stuffing)
one 10-ounce bottle Major Grey's chutney,
   or another kind of your favorite chutney, for serving
80 (1 package) round thin wonton wrappers

Season the salmon cubes on all sides with salt and pepper and refrigerate.

Heat 2 tablespoons of the peanut oil in a heavy-bottomed pan. Add the onions, apples, and chilies and cook over medium heat while stirring with a wooden spoon. After about 15 minutes, when the onions have softened, stir in the garlic, ginger, and curry powder and cook for 2 minutes more. Let cool and stir in the chopped cilantro. Season the mixture to taste with salt, oversalting slightly so it will be right when you add the salmon.

While you're cooking the onion mixture, chop the salmon to the consistency of hamburger relish by pulsing it in a food processor or by chopping it by hand with a chefs' knife. Stir it into the cool curry mixture.

Spread 2 tablespoons of oil on a sheet pan to keep the samosas from sticking as you construct them. Working one at a time, lightly brush a wonton wrapper with cold water and place a scant tablespoon of filling slightly to the right of the center. Fold one side of the wrapper over the filling and pinch the wrapper where the two halves meet, creating a seal. You should have a mound of filling, surrounded on the rounded side by a ¼ to ½ inch border of wrapper. Fold this border up against the mound to reinforce the seal. Put the samosas on the oiled sheet pan as you make them.

Heat the remaining oil in a heavy-bottomed pan or electric frying pan. When deep-frying, the oil should never come more than halfway up the sides of the pan. Put one of the samosas in the oil. The oil is at the right temperature when the samosa sinks for about 3 seconds and then rises back to the surface, surrounded with bubbles.

Fry the samosas, ¼ of the batch at a time, for about 2 minutes on each side— you may have to stir them a bit since they tend to flip and cook only on one side—until they are golden brown. Remove from the oil with a skimmer and drain on paper towels. Serve immediately with the chutney as an hors d'oeuvre.

Until I went to Mexico, I thought tacos were the kind I encountered growing up in California—crisp folded tortillas partially filled with ground beef and cheese. I've since discovered that tacos come in many forms and are only rarely stuffed with ground beef and cheese.

In Mexico, tacos are made by stuffing various ingredients such as stews, grilled meats (usually pork), and seafood into soft steamed tortillas. More often than not a variety of ingredients are passed around the table for guests to help themselves and design their own variations. Tacos are also fried—the raw tortillas are sautéed for a few seconds in hot oil, the taco is stuffed and rolled, and the whole thing is then deep-fried. My own preference is for the soft variety, partly because of the casualness of people making their own tacos, partly because they're less rich.

These salmon tacos are an obvious derivative of more traditional recipes, but the spirit of improvisation is authentic.

MAKES 12 TACOS, ENOUGH FOR 6 LIGHT OR
4 SUBSTANTIAL MAIN COURSES

1½ pounds salmon fillet with the skin and pin bones removed
salt
pepper
3 ripe avocados, preferably Hass
2 tablespoons lime juice (about 1 lime)
1 garlic clove, chopped fine and crushed to a paste with the side of a
   chefs' knife
12 corn tortillas
3 limes, cut into wedges
5 ripe tomatoes, peeled, seeded, and chopped (peeling and seeding optional)
leaves from 1 large bunch cilantro
5 jalapeño chilies, stemmed, seeded, and chopped fine
2 poblano chilies, charred, peeled, stemmed, seeded, and chopped (optional)
1 large red onion, halved through the root end, and sliced as thin as possible
1½ cups sour cream
1 small bunch lettuce, such as Romaine, leaves washed and dried,
   sliced into ¼-inch wide strips

Cut the salmon fillet into 3 pieces to make it easier to handle. Season the pieces on both sides with salt and pepper and refrigerate.

Peel and dice the avocados, gently toss with the lime juice and garlic paste, and season to taste with salt and pepper.

About 20 minutes before you're ready to serve, sprinkle each of the tortillas lightly with cold water by dipping your fingers into a bowl of water and then flicking the water on the tortillas. Wrap the tortillas in a clean kitchen towel and then tightly in aluminum foil and slide them into a 300° F oven.

Pat the salmon dry and grill it as described on page 57, hot smoke it as described on page 98, or sauté it as described on page 25.

When the salmon is cooked, cut it into ¾-inch cubes—don't worry if it crumbles a little—and put the cubes in a serving bowl.

Remove the foil from the tortillas—leave them in the towel—and put them on a heated plate.

Pass the tortillas, salmon, lime wedges, avocados, tomatoes, cilantro, chilies, onion, sour cream, and lettuce at the table in colorful bowls—or set them out if you're serving buffet style—and let guests roll up their own, choosing whatever ingredients they like.

CURING

Originally fish was cured to preserve it. Curing almost always requires salt and sometimes sugar, used either dry or dissolved in water to make brine. (Stockfish, which is air dried with neither salt nor sugar, is one of the rare exceptions.) Nowadays, curing is also used to enhance the flavor of all sorts of foods, not just seafood. But of all foods, with the possible exception of pork, salmon is almost always improved by some degree of curing. Curing removes moisture from salmon, enhances its flavor, makes it less likely to stick to a grill, and gives it a firmer, more toothsome texture. Salmon to be grilled, sautéed, or hot-smoked will always benefit from a 2-hour soaking in salt and sugar brine. Salmon that isn't going to be cooked is cured longer, usually with dry salt and sugar to give it a very firm texture (making it easy to cut into thin slices) and to season it throughout. This long curing is the method used for making gravlox (see page 94) or cold-smoked salmon (see page 102).

BRINE FOR GRILLED, SAUTÉED, OR HOT-SMOKED SALMON

This recipe makes enough brine to cure two whole salmon fillets. How much brine you need will depend on if you leave the fillets (or steaks) whole or cut them into pieces and on the shape of your container. Look for a non-reactive container that fits the salmon as closely as possible so that you need less brine. If you want to figure out in advance how much brine you need to make, arrange the fish in the container, pour in enough water to cover, and then measure the water.

MAKES ABOUT 3 QUARTS

4 cups salt
2 cups granulated sugar
10 cups water

Combine everything in a non-reactive pot and bring to a simmer. Stir to dissolve the salt and sugar. Let cool at room temperature for an hour and then refrigerate until well chilled.

Brining Salmon for Grilling, Sautéing, or Hot-Smoking: Soak thick salmon steaks or fillets in the cold brine in the refrigerator for 2 hours. Soak thinner fillets or escalopes for only 1 hour or they'll end up too salty. Drain and pat dry before grilling, sautéing, or hot smoking. Salmon that has been soaked in brine doesn't need any salt. The flesh will also stay more moist—even if you overcook it a little—and the salmon will be less likely to stick to the grill or sauté pan.

Dry-curing Salmon Fillets for Gravlox and Cold-Smoking: Because gravlox and cold-smoked salmon are never cooked, you have to cure them more than salmon you're going to grill, sauté, or hot-smoke. Instead of using brine, dry-curing involves coating salmon fillets with varying amounts of coarse salt and sugar for different lengths of time. Gravlox—Scandinavian-style cured salmon—is also cured with dill, but chefs today often replace it with another herb, such as tarragon (see also Cold-Smoked Salmon, page 102).

GRAVLOX

MAKES ENOUGH FOR 20 FIRST-COURSE SERVINGS
OR 40 HORS-D'OEUVRE SERVINGS

> **two 3- to 4-pound whole salmon fillets with the skin attached,** scaled
> **1 cup sugar**
> **1 cup coarse sea salt**
> **about 20 sprigs of dill or tarragon,** enough to cover generously
>   the top of one of the fillets
> **3 tablespoons chopped dill or tarragon leaves** (chopped at the last minute)
> **1 teaspoon olive oil** (if you're using tarragon instead of dill)

Pull the pin bones out of the salmon fillets (see page 19) and prepare a triple-thick layer of aluminum foil about 3 times the width and slightly longer than one of the fillets.

Combine the sugar and salt and spread ½ cup of the mixture along the length of the aluminum foil. Place one of the fillets, skin side down, on top of the mixture. Make sure the mixture is spread so the entire skin of the fillet touches some of the mixture. Rub another ½ cup of the mixture over the flesh side of the fillet, using slightly more mixture over the thick end. Place the dill or tarragon on top of the fillet so its entire surface is covered and gently spread another ½ cup of the sugar-salt mixture over it.

Place the second fillet, skin side up, on top of the first and rub it with the rest of the sugar-salt mixture. Fold up the sides of the aluminum foil so the fillets are tightly wrapped and place the packet on a sheet pan or cutting board large enough to hold it. Place another sheet pan or cutting board on top of the packet—again either one should run the length of the packet—and place a couple of cans or heavy-bottomed saucepans on top to gently weight the salmon. Put the whole contraption in the refrigerator for 48 hours. Turn the salmon over every 12 hours, being sure to put back the weights after each turn.

When the curing is done, unwrap the salmon fillets, quickly rinse them on both sides under cold running water, and pat them dry with paper towels. Smear the flesh side of both fillets with chopped dill or tarragon. If you're using tarragon, rub the leaves with olive oil (this keeps them from blackening) before you chop them. Wrap the fillets in plastic wrap and refrigerate them. They will keep for up to a week in the refrigerator. You can also freeze them for up to 3 months by first wrapping them in plastic wrap and then in a double layer of aluminum foil. Serve in thin slices (see box about slicing smoked salmon on page 104).

SMOKING

There are two kinds of smoking: hot-smoking and cold-smoking. When you hot-smoke salmon, you smoke and cook it at the same time. You can hot-smoke in one of two ways. For either method you should first cure the salmon in brine (see page 93). If you're smoking salmon to be served right away—a delicious way to cook salmon—it only needs 2 hours in brine and should be smoked just long enough to cook it through without drying it out. You should serve it while it's still hot. The second method, used for preserving the salmon and then serving it cold, requires a longer curing in brine—up to 24 hours—and then a longer and hotter smoking, to an internal temperature of 180° F. Because this second method always causes the salmon to dry out—especially if you're using Pacific salmon, which is leaner than Atlantic salmon—I never do it.

Cold-smoked salmon is exactly what it sounds like. The salmon is first dry-cured and then smoked away from the heat source, so the smoke isn't hot enough to cook it. You then serve the salmon, thinly sliced as you would gravlox, as an appetizer with blinis, with toasts, or as an ingredient in other recipes. Cold-smoked salmon is expensive to buy— about 5 times the price of raw salmon—so, despite being a bit complicated, it's worth making it yourself.

HOT-SMOKED SALMON FILLETS,
ESCALOPES, OR STEAKS

When I hot-smoke at home, I use one of three methods, depending on how much fish I'm smoking, the weather, and how ambitious I'm feeling. In the winter, when I'm smoking salmon for no more than 4 people, I use a stove-top smoker or wok. In the summer, for small amounts, I use a covered grill, which is probably the easiest way. If I'm smoking for a crowd, I use an electric smoker with racks about the size of a large oven (see sources, page 156). When I'm using the grill, stove-top smoker, or wok, I use wood chips; when I'm using the electric smoker, I use sawdust. Hot-smoked salmon is delicious served with the cucumber salsa on page 69 or the tropical salsa on page 71.

MAKES 4 MAIN-COURSE SERVINGS

> one 1½- to 2-pound salmon fillet, skin on or off and pin bones removed,
>   cut into 4 sections, or escalopes, or four 6- to 8-ounce salmon steaks
> ½ brine recipe (see page 93)
> 2 tablespoons olive oil
> 1 tablespoon vegetable oil
> wood chips (if you're using a covered barbecue, stove-top smoker, or wok)
>   or sawdust (if you're using an electric smoker) from fruitwood,
>   maple, grape vines, or mesquite (see sources, page 156)

Soak the salmon in the brine in the refrigerator for 2 hours and pat it dry. Don't soak for longer or you'll make the salmon too salty. If you're using wood chips and not sawdust, soak them in water for about 2 hours.

Covered Barbecue Method: Build a fire in the barbecue as though you were grilling, but instead of spreading the hot coals evenly under the rack, heap them up on one side. Makes sure the rack itself is perfectly clean and rub it with oil. Rub the salmon on both sides with olive oil. Put the wet wood chips on top of the coals. If you're cooking salmon with the skin on, arrange the salmon fillets, skin side down, over the coals and grill just long enough to crisp up the skin, about 3 minutes. Turn the salmon over—it won't stick because you brined it—placing it on a section of the rack *not* over the coals. If you're grilling skinned fillets, skip the initial grilling over the coals, and place the fillets, most attractive side up, on the rack not over the coals. Cover the grill and cook the salmon for about 10 minutes per inch of thickness and serve immediately, either plain, glazed, or with one of the sauces for grilled salmon.

Electric Smoker Method: Mine is made of sheet metal, has racks in it like an oven, and a hot plate on the bottom with a pan to hold smoldering sawdust. It's not as hot as a covered grill, so the smoking times tend to be longer—you'll have to check your salmon by feeling it (it should just begin to feel firm instead of fleshy) or by cutting a piece, which should have just a slight sheen near the center. I set my smoker on medium to high and let the sawdust smolder awhile—at first it has a strong acrid smell that should be burnt off for about 10 minutes—before you arrange the oiled salmon fillets or steaks on the racks.

Stove-Top Method: While there are inexpensive stove-top smokers on the market, you can improvise using either a pot or a wok. You'll need an old, heavy pot that you don't care terribly much about. An old-fashioned iron Dutch oven will also work. You'll also need a round cake rack as close to the size of the inside of the pot as possible and three empty cans all the same size, with both ends cut out. The size of the cans depends on the height of the pot. I use cat-food or tuna fish cans because my pot is rather low. Use soup cans for a tall pot.

Line the inside of the pot with extra heavy-duty aluminum foil or with a double layer of heavy duty aluminum foil with the shiny side facing toward the inside of the pot. Set the cans on end in the bottom of the pot, put 1½ cups of wood chips or sawdust in the bottom of the pot, and set the cake rack on top of the cans. Set the brined salmon, skin side down if you've left the skin on, on the rack. Cover the pot and put it on the stove over high heat (open the windows). Within 5 minutes, smoke should be leaking out rather abundantly from under the lid. Start timing when you see smoke and continue smoking for 10 minutes per inch of thickness of the salmon. If you hear spattering and there's too much smoke, turn down the heat. Check the salmon by feeling it or by cutting into a piece.

If you're using a wok, place the wood chips or sawdust over the bottom of the wok and place a double sheet of aluminum foil over the wood. Arrange a circular cake rack in the wok to hold the salmon. When the wood begins to smolder (over medium-high heat), place the salmon on the rack and the lid on the wok.

Stove-Top Smokers: My stove-top smoker is a rectangular stainless steel dish with a tray, a grill, and a cover. Spread wood chips that have been soaked for at least 2 hours on the bottom of the container, and place the tray, wrapped in aluminum foil to protect it, on top. Rub the grill lightly with oil. Placed the salmon, skin side down if you've left the skin on, on the grill. Slide the cover on and place the whole apparatus on the stove over high heat. You'll see smoke leaking out from under the lid after about 5 minutes. At this point, start timing the cooking, about 10 minutes of smoking per inch of thickness. When the time is up, turn off the heat, allow the smoker to cool and the smoke to dissipate, and remove the lid. Check the salmon by feeling it or by cutting into a piece.

HOT-SMOKED SALMON FILLETS WITH ORANGE GLAZE

Hot-smoked salmon's full flavor can be even better when the salmon is brushed during smoking with a savory glaze. These same glazes can also be used for grilled salmon, but since grilled salmon is turned midway during cooking, and the glaze is only brushed on after the salmon is turned, the flavor of the glaze is more subtle.

MAKES 4 MAIN-COURSE SERVINGS

four 6- to 8-ounce salmon fillets, skin on or off, and pin bones removed
½ **recipe brine** (see page 93)
1 orange
1 cup fresh orange juice
1½ **teaspoons sugar**
1 teaspoon fresh thyme or marjoram leaves, chopped fine, or
  ½ **teaspoon dried thyme leaves**
2 tablespoons balsamic vinegar
1 teaspoon cornstarch

Soak the salmon fillets in brine for 2 hours in the refrigerator.

Shave the zest off about half the orange in strips with a small paring knife, leaving as little of the white pith attached to the zests as possible. Cut the zest into very thin julienne strips or chop them fine. Squeeze the orange. Strain and save the juice.

Add the juice from the orange to the fresh orange juice, and combine with the orange zest, sugar, and thyme in a small saucepan. Bring to a simmer and cook it down until you're left with about ¼ cup of liquid. Remove from the heat and let cool.

Stir together the vinegar and cornstarch to get any lumps out of the cornstarch. Stir the cornstarch into the cooled orange mixture.

When you're ready to start smoking, bring the orange mixture to a simmer, stirring constantly, until it thickens. Put the salmon in the smoker (if you're smoking skin-on fillets in a covered barbecue, grill them skin side down directly over the coals for about 3 minutes to crisp the skin) and brush or spoon on the orange glaze with the zests. If you can't get all the glaze to cling to the top of the salmon, coat it again after smoking for 5 minutes.

HOT-SMOKED SALMON RILLETTES

Rillettes are a traditional French dish made by combining shredded cooked goose, pork, or duck with rendered fat and spices. While such a concoction may not sound terribly appetizing, there are few better things to spread on bread as a light snack or before dinner as an hors d'oeuvre. Lately, rillettes made out of seafood are appearing on menus in France and the United States. Shredded salmon is combined with crème fraîche, whipped cream, or homemade mayonnaise. Because of its full flavor, I like to use hot-smoked salmon. Salmon rillettes keep for up to 3 days in the refrigerator.

MAKES 2 CUPS (ENOUGH FOR 6 HORS-D'OEUVRE SERVINGS)

1 pound skinless hot-smoked salmon, chilled
½ cup crème fraîche, homemade mayonnaise (see recipe page 65),
 or heavy cream beaten until it mounds up but not until stiff
1 small shallot, chopped very fine (optional)
1 clove garlic, chopped fine and crushed to a paste with the side
 of a chefs' knife (optional)
salt
pepper
toasted country bread, for serving

Shred the salmon by crushing it with your fingers. Work it with the back of a fork in a mixing bowl with the crème fraîche, homemade mayonnaise, or heavy cream. Work in the optional shallot and garlic. Season to taste with salt and pepper. Serve chilled with toasted country bread.

COLD-SMOKED SALMON

I'll say it right off the bat: this is a bit of a project and, as one of my editors once told me, it's kind of a "guy thing." But it's a fun project that makes wonderful smoked salmon that will thrill your guests and be a lot cheaper—and usually better—than anything you can buy. Before you embark on this project, I must warn you that it's something you should do outside.

With cold-smoking, you need to generate smoke as you do when hot-smoking, but you must also make sure the smoke is cool—or at least not burning hot—when it comes in contact with the salmon so the salmon does not cook. Commercial salmon smokers fill whole rooms with smoke, and the size of the room and the distance of the salmon from the heat source prevent the salmon from cooking. Restaurants sometimes use smaller commercial cold smokers, but they cost a fortune. The equipment for my improvised method costs about the same as 4 fillets of good quality store-bought smoked salmon.

MAKES ENOUGH FOR 20 FIRST-COURSE SERVINGS
OR 40 HORS-D'OEUVRE SERVINGS

> **two 3- to 4-pound salmon fillets with the skin on,** scaled
> **2 cups coarse salt**
> **2 cups granulated sugar**
> **about 6 cups hardwood sawdust**

Curing the Salmon: Salmon that is going to be cold-smoked needs to be cured more completely than gravlox, and it is cured in two stages instead of one. Prepare a triple-thick layer of foil about 3 times the width and slightly longer than one of the fillets. Spread ½ cup of the salt along the length of the foil and place one of the fillets, skin side down, on top of the salt. Make sure the salt is spread so the entire skin touches some of the salt. Rub a cup of the salt over the flesh side of the fillet, using slightly more over the thick end of the fillet. Place the second fillet, skin side up, on top of the first and rub it with the rest of the salt. Fold up the sides of the foil so the fillets are tightly wrapped and place the packet on a sheet pan or cutting board large enough to hold the fillets. Place another sheet pan or cutting board on top of the fillets equal-sized and place a couple of cans or heavy-bottomed saucepans on top to gently weight the salmon. Put the whole contraption in the refrigerator for 20 hours. Turn the salmon over after 10 hours, then replace the weights.

Unwrap the salmon fillets and quickly rinse them under cold water. Pat them dry with paper towels. Rinse the salt off the foil and pat it dry with paper towels. Repeat the curing, this time using the sugar, for 20 hours, turning the salmon over after 10 hours. Rinse the sugar off the fillets and pat them dry. Wrap tightly in plastic wrap and refrigerate, up to 3 days, until you're ready to smoke.

Rigging Up a Cold-Smoker: First you must buy an electric smoker (see sources on page 156). When it arrives, save the cardboard box it comes in—this becomes the actual smoking chamber, which you can use again and again. There will also be some cardboard packing materials that you should also save. Next, you need to make a trip to the hardware store to buy some stovepipe and duct tape. Get 2 stovepipe elbows and 3 lengths of stovepipe, one 3-foot-long piece and two 1-foot-long pieces.

The day you're ready to smoke the cured salmon (which should be at least a day before you plan on serving the salmon), twist off the chimney that comes out of the top of the smoker and in its place twist in one of the 1-foot lengths of stovepipe. Twist one of the elbows onto the top of the pipe. Set the cardboard box, open end up, next to the smoker. Tape the cardboard packing materials along the 4 inside corners of the box so the tops come about half way up the sides of the box—these are the supports for the rack. Take one of the metal racks out of the smoker and place it in the cardboard box on the ends of the cardboard packing materials so the rack is resting about half way down in the box.

Cut a flap on one side of the box, at the bottom—like a small cat door—about 6 inches wide and 8 inches high and open it a couple of inches. This will allow the smoke to escape.

When you're ready to smoke, cut a half circle out of each of the top flaps of the box so they join together and form a circle in the center, using the end of a piece of stovepipe as a guide. Put two cured salmon fillets, skin side down, diagonally on top of the rack—if they don't fit exactly, just bend them up onto the sides of the cardboard. Fold down the top cardboard flaps—use some duct tape to hold them down—and twist a 1-foot length of stovepipe into the hole on top of the box. Seal it around with duct tape and twist on an elbow pipe.

You will now have the metal smoker and a cardboard box, both with pipe sticking out the top with an elbow pipe attached to it. Now connect the two pipes with the 3-foot length of stovepipe.

Using the Cold-Smoker: Put about 2 cups of sawdust in the small metal pan on the hot plate in the metal smoker. Slide down the metal door but put something under it so it doesn't quite close all the way, with about an inch of space to allow air in. Set the hot plate between medium and high. After about 10 minutes, you should notice smoke coming out of the flap at the bottom of the cardboard smoking chamber. Feel the pipe that leads from the oven to the chamber. If it feels hot, turn down the hot plate—you don't want the smoke to cook the salmon.

After about 30 minutes you'll notice that no more smoke is being produced. Add another 2 cups of sawdust to the hot pan. Keep adding sawdust to the pan—you'll need to discard the hot coals in the pan every hour or so when the pan fills up and the coals no longer produce smoke—whenever you notice that no more smoke is being produced, about every half hour. Smoke the salmon for a total of 4 hours.

Finishing the Smoked Salmon: When the salmon is smoked, set it in front of a fan for about 2 hours to dry it out slightly and cause a skin to form on its surface. If possible, do this outside in the shade. In the winter, I set the salmon in the opened, turned-off oven and set a square window fan directly in front of it. Your house will smell like smoke for a couple of days, which isn't entirely unpleasant. Wrap the salmon fillets separately in plastic wrap and refrigerate them for 24 hours to allow the smoke flavor to penetrate the fillets.

Serving Smoked Salmon and Gravlox: Slicing a whole smoked salmon fillet in thin, elegant slices takes a little practice but once you master it you can serve your smoked salmon in front of guests in the dining room—something that never fails to impress. You'll also need a special knife. The best knife, sometimes called a smoked salmon slicer or a ham slicer, has a long, flat, flexible blade. In a pinch you can also use a long carving knife—provided it has some flexibility—or a long, thin fish-filleting knife.

First, trim the thin leathery skin from the surface of the part of the salmon you're going to serve (which can be the whole thing if you're serving a crowd). Be sure to trim the sides of the salmon. Pull out the pin bones—you can also remove them before smoking, but they come out more easily when the salmon has been cured and smoked. Assuming you're right-handed, set the salmon on a large cutting board or flat platter with the tail facing away from you at about 2 o'clock. Start slicing about ⅓ up from the tail. To make thin slices you must press the knife against the salmon so the blade actually bends a little and then slide the knife toward the tail, watching the blade cut through the salmon (the salmon is slightly translucent), regulating the thickness of the slice by making minute changes in the angle of the knife. Keep repeating this, starting about ¼ inch farther back for each slice. The salmon gets easier to slice as you get farther along, because the flesh is denser and less likely to crumble.

Transfer the slices to large plates with the side of the slicing knife.

POACHING

To poach is to cook covered in hot liquid. It differs from boiling because when poaching, the liquid is kept at a bare simmer. Cooking fish in boiling liquid quickly dries it out and causes it to fall apart. Poaching differs from braising in the amount of liquid used. Poached salmon is completely submerged in hot liquid, while braised salmon (or any other fish) is cooked with only enough liquid to come halfway (or less) up its sides.

The most important thing to remember when poaching is not to let the poaching liquid really boil. You also need to know whether or not to start poaching in cold liquid or in liquid that's already simmering. I poach whole salmon starting in cold liquid, so the outside of the salmon doesn't overcook by the time the heat penetrates to the center. By starting in cold liquid that is slowly brought to a simmer with the fish in it, the heat penetrates the salmon slowly so it cooks evenly. If I'm poaching smaller pieces of salmon, such as steaks or fillets, I slip them in already simmering liquid. If I were to start them in cold liquid, they would overcook and dry out before the liquid even reached a simmer.

Most of us associate poached salmon with the whole, cold poached salmon served at buffets. A whole poached salmon, hot or cold, is indeed a lovely thing, but some people are intimidated by making one because most recipes insist you need a fish poacher, a rather expensive piece of kitchen equipment you may not want to buy for those few times when you poach whole large fish. But having a fish poacher does make life easy because it has a rack that you can use for lifting the fish out of the poaching liquid. If you don't have a poacher, follow the directions on page 110).

VEGETABLE BROTH FOR POACHING SALMON

The usual poaching liquid for most seafood, what the French call a court bouillon, is little more than a simple vegetable broth made with onions, carrots, celery, some herbs, and white wine. You don't have to use all these ingredients—I sometimes just use onions and the herbs—and you don't have to tie the herbs up in a bouquet garni because the vegetable broth doesn't need to be skimmed. The whole thing is just strained and the vegetables, having given their all to the surrounding liquid, are thrown out. If you're disturbed by buying a whole bunch of celery when you only need a few branches, wrap the rest tightly in aluminum foil and freeze it. It will loose its texture—you won't be able to serve it raw—but its flavor stays intact so you can use it for making broths and soups. The recipe given here is for a whole salmon—much more than twice what you'll need if you're poaching salmon steaks or fillets.

MAKES 8 QUARTS (ENOUGH TO POACH A WHOLE 7-POUND
SALMON, 12 TO 14 MAIN-COURSE SERVINGS)

10 medium onions (about 5 pounds), peeled, halved through the root end, and sliced about ⅛-inch thick

12 medium carrots (about 5 pounds without the greens), peeled, halved lengthwise, and sliced about ⅛-inch thick

6 stalks of celery (about 1 pound), sliced about ⅛-inch thick

2 large bunches of parsley

6 imported bay leaves

20 sprigs of fresh thyme or 2 teaspoons dried thyme leaves

1 bottle dry white wine

salt

Combine the onions, carrots, celery, parsley, bay leaves, and thyme in a large pot—or divide everything into two pots if you don't have one that's big enough—and pour over 8 quarts of water. Cover the pot and bring to a boil over high heat. When the water boils, turn down the heat and simmer gently, partially covered, for 40 minutes. Add the wine and salt and simmer for 15 minutes more. Strain the broth and discard the vegetables. Let the broth cool and refrigerate until needed, up to a week.

POACHING WHOLE SALMON IN A FISH POACHER

If you have a fish poacher, poaching a whole salmon is a snap. You just set the fish on the rack, pour over enough cold poaching liquid to cover, put on the lid, and set the poacher on the stove so it spans two burners. Turn the heat to between medium and high, ideally just the right amount of heat so the liquid approaches a boil at the same time the salmon is done, about 45 minutes. If you're going out to buy a fish poacher for salmon, buy the largest one you can find—mine is 24 inches long, which seems to be a standard and is just large enough to hold a 7-pound salmon with the head and tail attached.

MAKES ENOUGH FOR 12 TO 14 MAIN-COURSE SERVINGS (MORE IF OTHER ITEMS ARE BEING SERVED AT A BUFFET)

> **1 whole 8-pound salmon,** gutted, scaled, and gills removed
> **1 recipe cool vegetable broth** (see page 107)

Set the salmon in a large fish poacher. If you suddenly discover that your poacher isn't large enough, cut off the head and trim the tail. If you still can't get it into the poacher, poach it in the oven following the recipe on page 110.

Pour the vegetable broth over the salmon—if it doesn't completely cover the salmon, just add enough water to cover or continually baste the part of the salmon that protrudes above the surface—put on the lid, and set the fish poacher on the stove so it spans two burners. Turn the heat to between medium and high, cover the poacher, and poach the salmon for about 45 minutes. If after 20 minutes the liquid hasn't approached the simmer (it doesn't steam and there's not a single bubble), turn up the heat. If the liquid starts to boil, turn it down to maintain it at a bare simmer.

Regardless of how you cook a whole salmon—whether you poach it in a fish poacher or in the oven, or you grill or roast it—you can use the same method to determine if it's done. The easiest method is to stick an instant-read thermometer into the back of the fish, approaching from the back side parallel to the backbone. When the thermometer reads 125° F, the salmon is ready to remove from the heat. (It's done at 135° F, but it will continue to cook on the inside as the heat penetrates into the middle.) If you don't have a thermometer, slide a small paring knife into the fish, again parallel to the backbone, and gently lift the knife. If the top fillet pulls away from the bone and doesn't cling or look raw on the inside near the central backbone, the salmon is ready.

Once the salmon is done, you've got to coax it onto a serving platter. (You should always present it whole because it's so dramatic.) At this point you may want to enlist one of your guests to help you lift the salmon out of the poacher. If the handles to the poaching rack are submerged, lift them up, one at a time, with the handles of two wooden spoons—this is where a helper comes in handy—and deftly slide the fish onto a heated platter. At this point, peel the skin off the top of the salmon with your fingers—it will come off easily if you remove it right away—and bring the salmon into the dining room for carving. If you're serving the salmon cold, cover it with plastic wrap; let it cool for an hour at room temperature, and then let it cool in the refrigerator for an hour. (You can also chill it all day, but salmon is better served just slightly cool than ice cold.)

To serve the salmon, hot or cold, slide a knife along the center of the fillet—which is easy to see because there will be a dark line running the length of the salmon in the center—all the way to the backbone. Slide a serving knife (ideally an offset fish knife) between the top fillet and the backbone, loosening but not detaching the top fillet. Then make cuts crosswise along the top of the salmon with a sharp boning knife or chef's knife. Make the cuts any size you like. Gently detach the fillets and place them on plates at the buffet. You can also let guests help themselves, but if you do, make the cuts and loosen the fillets ahead of time so they don't make a complete mess out of your fish. When the top fillet is completely gone, lift off the backbone and ribs and discard them along with the head. Because the inside of the bottom fillet is exposed, you'll be able to pull away any rib bones that are attached near the head of the fish and pull out any pin bones. Serve the bottom fillet in the same way—in crosswise slices. If you weren't able to remove the skin, do your best to leave it sticking to the platter. See the photos on page 111.

"POACHING" A WHOLE SALMON
WITHOUT A FISH POACHER

I got this idea from an article by Mark Bittman that appeared a few years ago in *Cook's Illustrated*, a magazine whose editors test and test until they get things just right. Mr. Bittman's method really consists of *baking* the salmon, but because it is first wrapped in aluminum foil, it actually steams—with results virtually identical to poaching—instead of ending up roasted (see page 125), which is something altogether different. The only thing you don't want to do is to buy a whole salmon and find that it's too big for your oven when you get home. So measure your oven—keeping in mind that you can place the salmon in the oven diagonally— before you shop.

MAKES 14 TO 16 MAIN-COURSE SERVINGS

> **1 whole 10-pound salmon** (or whatever size will fit in your oven),
>   gutted, scaled, and gills removed
> **2 tablespoons olive oil**
> **fine sea salt**
> **pepper**

Preheat the oven to 250° F.

Prepare a double-thick sheet of heavy-duty aluminum foil large enough to wrap the fish with a few inches left over and an extra 8 inches of foil on both the head and tail ends. Rub it with a tablespoon of olive oil. Rub the salmon with the rest of the oil and season it on both sides with salt and pepper. Bring the aluminum foil up around the sides of the salmon and seal the two edges of foil together, creating a seam that runs the length of the salmon. Fold the foil on the tail and head ends several times to create a seal. The idea is to seal the foil as best you can while still leaving a small amount of air inside with the salmon.

Arrange the salmon on a sheet pan or, if you don't have one big enough, directly on the middle oven rack. You may need to arrange the salmon diagonally.

Cooking fish in a low oven—one that simulates the temperature of poaching liquid—takes a lot longer than poaching in a fish poacher, usually about 2½ hours for a 10-pound salmon. To be on the safe side, start checking the doneness of the salmon after about 1½ hours by sticking an instant-read thermometer along the backbone of the salmon straight through the aluminum foil. It should read 130° F. If you don't have a thermometer, stick a metal skewer into the back of the salmon and immediately touch it to your bottom lip. When it feels distinctly warm, check the doneness of the salmon by running a knife along one side of the backbone—at this point it won't hurt to cut through the foil—and making sure that the flesh isn't raw inside next to the center backbone and that you can separate the flesh from the bones with the knife. If the flesh adheres to the bones, continue baking.

Gently unwrap the salmon, peel away its skin, and transfer it to a platter. Serve the salmon as described on page 109.

Removing skin from hot poached salmon.

Cutting down to backbone along center of top fillet.

Removing individual servings from top fillet.

Pulling away the backbone.

POACHED INDIVIDUAL SALMON
STEAKS, MEDALLIONS, OR FILLETS

While they may not make as dramatic a presentation, pieces of salmon are much easier to manage than whole salmon. You need far less poaching liquid and you don't need any special equipment—you can use a sauté pan with straight sides or a low-sided pot. For the poaching liquid you can use the traditional vegetable broth (court-bouillon, see recipe on page 107) or just some salted water simmered for about 10 minutes with a bouquet garni of parsley, bay leaves, and thyme. Steaks are best tied up into medallions (see page 20), so the stomach flaps don't overcook, and then poached with their skin on. Pull the skin off—it slips away easily—after cooking. (Unlike grilled or sautéed salmon skin, poached salmon skin has an unpleasant texture and consistency.) Salmon fillets are best poached with the skin off.

MAKES 4 MAIN-COURSE SERVINGS

> **four 6- to 8-ounce salmon fillets or steaks**
> **salt**
> **pepper**
> **½ recipe (4 quarts) vegetable broth, or 2 teaspoons**
>   **salt and a bouquet garni containing 1 bunch parsley, 3 imported bay**
>   **leaves, and 5 sprigs fresh thyme or ½ teaspoon dried thyme leaves**
> **lemon wedges**
> **extra-virgin olive oil**

Season the salmon with salt and pepper and refrigerate it for at least 30 minutes and up to several hours.

If you're not using the vegetable broth, simmer 4 quarts of water with the salt and bouquet garni in a straight-sided sauté pan or low-sided pot just large enough to hold the salmon in a single layer, for about 15 minutes.

If you have salmon steaks, you can poach them as they are but they'll cook more evenly if you turn them into medallions. Shortly before you're ready to serve, slide the salmon steaks, medallions, or fillets into the simmering liquid and poach them for about 9 minutes per inch of thickness. Transfer them to a hot plate with a spatula. If you've poached medallions, cut away the string. Pull the skin off the medallions or steaks and serve the salmon on hot plates. Pass the lemon wedges and olive oil, in a small pitcher, at the table.

Sauces to Serve with Poached Salmon

I usually enhance poached salmon with some kind of sauce. Unlike grilled or sautéed salmon, which has a more assertive flavor and is great served with a powerful sauce, poached salmon is best served with something delicate. Hot poached salmon is great with buttery and creamy sauces, which can be thinned to almost broth-like consistency by combining them with some of the poaching liquid. Probably the most classic sauce for hot poached salmon, hollandaise, never goes unappreciated. It is even better when lightened just before serving with a little whipped cream. Hollandaise is also a sauce you can play around with by adding ingredients of your own. I especially like to add chopped tarragon and parsley, so it resembles béarnaise sauce. Cold poached salmon can be served with any of the mayonnaises on pages 66 to 68, but I like to lighten the texture and flavor of these mayonnaises by combining them with whipped cream—about 1 cup heavy cream, whipped, per cup of mayonnaise. You'll need to readjust the seasoning.

You can also serve flavored butters—made by combining butter with chopped herbs or other flavorful ingredients—with hot poached salmon, or you can whip the butter in a mixer with a whisk attachment and then pass the butter at the table for guests to help themselves. You can also whisk any one (or several) of these flavored butters into a small amount of the hot salmon poaching liquid, combined with a little cream to keep the butter from separating.

FLAVORED BUTTERS FOR
HOT POACHED SALMON

Parsley and Lemon Butter: Chop the leaves from 1 bunch parsley and blend with ¼ pound softened butter in a mixing bowl with a heavy wooden spoon or in an electric mixer with the paddle blade. When the parsley is well incorporated, blend in two teaspoons of lemon juice.

Tarragon Butter: Rub 3 heaping tablespoons of fresh tarragon leaves with a teaspoon of olive oil (to prevent blackening) and chop fine. Blend the tarragon with ¼ pound butter by hand or with an electric mixer.

Dried Mushroom Butter: Rinse ½ cup dried morels or porcini in a strainer under cold running water and combine the mushrooms with ¼ cup cold water for 30 minutes. Stir the mushrooms around in the water every ten minutes so they soak up the water evenly. Squeeze the mushrooms—save the liquid that comes out— and chop them fine. Blend them with ¼ pound butter by hand or with an electric mixer. Blend in a tablespoon of the soaking liquid, leaving any grit behind in the bowl.

Whipped Butters: Whip any flavored butter in an electric mixer with the whisk attachment until it is light and fluffy. If you want a slightly warm and foamy butter, whisk in 2 tablespoons of the hot salmon poaching liquid per ¼ pound of butter just before serving.

Mounted Butter Sauces: When you whisk cold butter into a small amount of liquid, you end up with a creamy butter sauce. The best known of these sauces is beurre blanc, made by first cooking down a mixture of vinegar, white wine, and shallots and then whisking in butter. You can create your own mounted butter sauces by starting with different concentrated liquids (boiling down some of the poaching liquid from the salmon makes a great sauce) and then whisking in regular butter or a butter you've flavored with herbs, mushrooms, or other flavorful ingredients.

TARRAGON BUTTER SAUCE OR
TARRAGON AND MUSHROOM SAUCE
FOR POACHED SALMON

You can make any amount of this sauce by adjusting the amount of each ingredient accordingly.

ENOUGH FOR 8 MAIN-COURSE SERVINGS

2 cups vegetable broth (see page 107), or salmon poaching liquid
1 shallot or small onion, peeled, and chopped very fine
½ **cup heavy cream**
¼ **pound tarragon butter** (see page 114), cold, cut into 4 pieces
   or 4 tablespoons tarragon butter and 4 tablespoons
   dried mushroom butter (see page 114)
salt
pepper

Boil down the vegetable broth or salmon poaching liquid to about 1 cup, add the shallot, and boil down to about half again so you end up with ½ cup of sauce base. Pour in the heavy cream, boil it for about 30 seconds, and whisk in the cold butter. Season to taste with salt and pepper.

SERVING
RAW
SALMON

take a rather blithe approach to eating raw things from the sea, so if it looks and smells okay I go ahead and eat it. But occasionally salmon, especially wild salmon, may have parasites, and salmon that has been carelessly handled may have bacteria on its surface. I avoid the bacteria problem by only buying salmon from a clean fish store and handling the salmon carefully when I get it home (I clean my cutting boards, knives, and hands with hot water with bleach in it. If the bleach leaves your hands feeling slippery, rub them with vinegar.) Parasites are more difficult to kill because they live inside the salmon flesh. Experts recommend freezing salmon to be eaten raw, cold smoked, or cured, at -4° F for 7 days. If you're freezer isn't cold enough, buy salmon from someone you can trust and make sure it has been deep-frozen—ask for "frozen at sea" salmon, sometimes called FAS—or wrap it tightly in plastic wrap and aluminum foil in the freezer for 3 days.

SALMON TARTARE

I serve salmon tartare somewhat differently than classic steak tartare. I dispense with the raw egg yolks and instead serve homemade herb and caper mayonnaise, extra capers, and mustard. I chop the raw salmon with a chefs' knife, but a food processor will also work.

MAKES 6 FIRST-COURSE SERVINGS

> 1 to 1½ pounds salmon fillet with the skin, pin bones, and dark patches removed
> 1 recipe homemade herb and caper mayonnaise (see page 68)
> 6 tablespoons capers (preferably the small non pareils kind)
> whole-grain mustard

Cut the salmon into cubes about ¼ inch on each side using a chefs' knife, or by pulsing briefly in a food processor.

Just before you're ready to serve, spoon a mound of salmon in the center of 6 chilled plates or glasses. Pass the tartar sauce, capers, and mustard for guests to mix into the salmon tartare to taste.

SALMON CARPACCIO WITH EXTRA-VIRGIN OLIVE OIL AND BALSAMIC VINEGAR

The time-consuming part of this dish can be done earlier the day you plan to serve it. Just cover the individual plates with plastic wrap, stack them in pairs, and keep them in the refrigerator. Use the best balsamic vinegar you can afford.

MAKES 6 FIRST-COURSE SERVINGS

1½ pounds salmon fillet with the skin on and any pin bones removed
that has been frozen (see page 117), from the tail end, in one piece
3 tablespoons good quality balsamic vinegar
2 teaspoons salt, preferably sea salt
¼ cup extra-virgin olive oil
15 fresh basil leaves
3 tablespoons salmon roe or caviar (optional)

Slice the salmon into thin slices as you would smoked salmon by pressing a flexible knife against the salmon, in the middle of the fillet, so the blade actually bends a little. Then slide the knife toward the tail while holding your left hand against the salmon to keep the flesh compact and make it easier to slice. Lift your hand up every few seconds so you can see the blade through the salmon and regulate the thickness of the slices by making minute changes in the angle of the knife. Keep repeating this, starting about an inch farther back for each slice. Don't worry if your pieces are small or irregular—slicing raw salmon thin takes some practice and small pieces will still look good on the plate.

Arrange the salmon slices on chilled plates. You can arrange the slices so the center of the plate is completely covered or you can trim the slices and arrange them on the plate to form a perfect rectangle. Don't overlap the slices.

Combine the vinegar and salt in a small bowl. Rub the basil leaves with a teaspoon of olive oil—to keep them from turning dark during chopping—and chop them just before serving. Combine the chopped basil and the rest of the olive oil with the vinegar-salt mixture. Drizzle the mixture over the salmon on each plate. Arrange tiny mounds of salmon roe or caviar on each serving and serve immediately.

One of my favorite meals is a lunch or dinner eaten sitting at a sushi bar in front of a display case filled with sparkling fresh fish and peculiar looking squiggly things. I don't indulge in such a meal lightly, because when I do I leave the decisions up to the sushi chef, a tactic that almost always ensures marvelous food but also an exorbitant check. I eat alone or with one other person, because conversation at a sushi bar between more than two people is awkward and distracting from the goodies at hand. In better places, usually sometime in the middle of the meal, the sushi chef offers me a hand roll that is shaped like an ice cream cone but with seaweed *(nori)* replacing the cone and raw or cool cooked fish, rice, and cucumber replacing the ice cream.

12 HAND ROLLS WILL MAKE 12 HORS-D'OEUVRE OR
SNACK PORTIONS OR 6 HORS-D'OEUVRE PORTIONS
IF NO OTHER HORS D'OEUVRES ARE BEING SERVED

1 long hothouse cucumber or 2 regular cucumbers, peeled, cut in half lengthwise, and seeds scooped out with a spoon
6 tablespoons Japanese soy sauce
six 8 x 7 inch rectangles *nori*, a standard size
1 pound grilled, broiled, raw, or hot-smoked salmon fillet
2 teaspoons wasabi powder (see sources, page 156)
1 recipe sushi rice (see page 123)

Cut the cucumber halves lengthwise into ¼-inch thick strips. Slice these so you end up with ¼-inch cubes. Toss these in a mixing bowl with 2 tablespoons soy sauce and allow to drain for an hour in a colander.

Cut the *nori* rectangles in half crosswise so you end up with twelve 4 x 7-inch rectangles.

Cut the salmon into ½-inch cubes. If you're using raw salmon, cut it into ¼-inch cubes. Combine half the wasabi with 1 tablespoon of water and blend it to a smooth paste—be careful, the fumes will knock your head back. Gently combine the wasabi with the salmon, a little bit at a time, to taste—I use my fingers so I don't break up the salmon. Combine the remaining wasabi with the remaining soy sauce to use as a dipping sauce.

Put the cucumber in a kitchen towel (well rinsed out to eliminate traces of soap) and wring it out as hard as you can to eliminate liquid.

Place a rectangle of *nori* on the work surface in front of you with the long side facing you. Place a heaping tablespoon of rice diagonally, starting an inch away from the upper right corner and ending about an inch away from the middle of the *nori* rectangle. Spoon a tablespoon of cucumber over it and press the cucumber gently into the rice. Arrange the salmon next to the rice, near the upper right corner. Fold the bottom left corner of *nori* over the rice, and tuck it in slightly under the rice. (Dip your fingers in cold water as you work to keep the rice from sticking to them.) Roll the *nori* into a cone and hand it to one of your guests. Make them one at a time, handing them to your guests as you go, with the dipping sauce nearby.

Raw sushi rice with nori.

Sushi Rice: To make any kind of sushi, you first need to make seasoned rice. There's nothing difficult about this as long as you forget everything you've learned about cooking rice. First, you must use Japanese sushi rice (see sources, page 156), which is a starchy medium-grain rice that holds together once cooked. To make slightly more than 2 cups cooked sushi rice—more than enough for 12 hand rolls—thoroughly rinse 1 cup sushi rice by running cold water over it in a strainer. Put it in a heavy-bottomed pot with 1 cup cold water. Place the pot over medium to high heat. When the water starts to simmer, cover the pot and turn the heat down to low. Cook the rice for 10 minutes—don't lift the lid at any point—and turn off the heat. Let the rice rest for 15 minutes, still without opening the lid.

While the rice is cooking, place 3 tablespoons good-quality rice vinegar (I use Kikkoman brand), 1½ tablespoons granulated sugar, and 2 teaspoons salt in a saucepan over low heat and stir until the salt and sugar dissolve. Dump the rice into a large mixing bowl and sprinkle the vinegar over it while tossing—not stirring or you'll make it gummy—the rice with a large wooden spoon or spatula. Cover the rice with plastic wrap and let it cool to room temperature before using it.

ROASTING
AND BAKING

In the strictest sense, roasting is cooking on a spit in front of an open fire. While I have succeeded in rigging up a spit in front of fireplaces at summer rentals—usually involving impaling a chicken or small fish on a long tree branch—I can't imagine how someone would spit-roast a salmon. But since most of us don't have spits, improvised or otherwise, we roast in the oven. So what's the difference between roasting and baking? Because I've never seen the two terms contrasted anywhere, I define them according to desired effect. Baking simply means cooking in the oven until cooked through, but roasting implies using high heat so whatever is being roasted ends up with a crisp brown crust. When roasting salmon—either a whole fish or a large cross-section, the trick is to get the skin to turn crisp without over- or under-cooking the fish. The thinner the salmon (or salmon section), the hotter the oven needs to be so the skin will crisp up before the fish overcooks. If the salmon or salmon section is very thick, it should roast in a medium oven so the heat can penetrate to the center before the skin burns. Giving exact directions on how to do this is next to impossible because everyone's oven is different, oven thermostats are unreliable, and it's very hard to come up with a salmon the exact weight you need for a particular recipe. The most reliable approach is to start out in a fairly hot oven—say 400° F—and when the salmon skin starts to turn crisp, turn the oven down to 300° F to continue cooking the salmon without burning the skin.

SALMON *EN PAPILLOTE* WITH SHIITAKE MUSHROOMS

Baking is a convenient way to cook salmon because you can do other things (including being with your guests) while it's cooking. Cooking *en papillote*, just a stylish way of describing baking in a paper bag, will provide you with another easy baking method because everything is put in the bag ahead of time and baked at the last minute. The guests can then amuse themselves by cutting open their own bags. (You can also bake a larger piece of salmon—more than one serving—and then cut it into pieces and place it on plates at the table.) Cooking en papillote is also a good method when you're using aromatic ingredients such as fresh herbs, wild mushrooms, or truffles, whose aroma may be lost if cooked in other ways.

Fish baked en papillote cooks faster than most baked fish because the fish actually steams.

MAKES 6 MAIN-COURSE SERVINGS

> **six 6-to 8-ounce salmon fillets with the skin and pin bones removed,**
>   all the same size
> **salt**
> **pepper**
> **18 large shiitake mushrooms,** stems removed (about 1½ pounds)
> **2 tablespoons butter**
> **1 shallot,** peeled, and finely chopped
> **1 small clove garlic,** finely chopped
> **12 tablespoons dry white wine**
> **6 tablespoons butter or 3 tablespoons porcini butter** (see page 114)
>   **and 3 tablespoons tarragon butter** (see page 114)
> **1 egg white,** if using parchment paper

Season the salmon fillets with salt and pepper.

Sauté the shiitake caps in butter over medium heat—don't let the butter burn—for about 10 minutes, stirring occasionally. Sprinkle the mushrooms with shallots, garlic, salt, and pepper after about 5 minutes. Reserve the mushrooms.

Cut 6 squares of parchment paper or aluminum foil about 16 x 12 inches. Fold the squares in half down the middle (like a book), unfold them, and place a slice of salmon just to the left of center of the right fold. Spoon 3 shiitake caps over each piece of salmon, and place a tablespoon of butter (or ½ tablespoon each of the flavored butters) over the salmon. Sprinkle each serving with 2 tablespoons of white wine.

If you're using parchment, combine the egg white with a teaspoon of salt and beat it with a fork for about a minute to loosen it. Brush the egg white around an inch-wide border of the squares and fold the squares over, pressing against the egg white to create an airtight seal. Brush the outer rim of the squares a second time with egg white and make a series of straight folds to make an airtight seal. Brush one last time with egg wash and set the papillotes on a sheet pan. If you're using aluminum foil, fold in the same way but don't bother with the egg whites.

Preheat the oven to 450° F and bake the papillotes on a baking sheet until they puff up, about 10 minutes per inch of thickness. Immediately slide the papillotes onto hot soup plates and serve.

Raw ivory salmon fillet.

WHOLE SALMON BAKED IN SALT

When I first read about a recipe for a whole fish baked in salt, I was skeptical, suspecting the salt was for show and little else. But with a little experimenting, I did find that the salt enhances the flavor of fish, and cracking open the hardened salt casing has a dramatic effect at the table.

The easiest way to enclose a whole fish in salt is to use an oval baking dish a few inches longer and wider than the fish, fill it with about a third of the salt mixture, place the fish on top, pack the rest of the salt over it, and set the whole thing on a sheet pan in a 400° F oven.

Because my oval baking dish isn't large, I only bake a whole salmon when I can find one that will fit—which means no more than 5 pounds. Since most farmed salmon are at least 8 pounds, you may have to order a small one or keep a look-out for so-called pink salmon, which is smaller and often a bargain (see page 13). If you want to bake a larger salmon, measure your largest sheet pan to make sure the fish will fit and then wrap the fish and salt with a triple layer of aluminum foil instead of baking it in a dish. Count on 1½ times as much salt (by weight) than fish and make sure that the fish is enclosed on all sides by at least a ½ -inch-thick layer of salt crust—you shouldn't see the fish through the salt. Use coarse salt—I use kosher salt because it's cheap.

MAKES 6 TO 10 MAIN-COURSE SERVINGS

one 5- to 7-pound whole salmon, scaled, gutted, and gills removed
6 or more egg whites, as needed
7 to 10 pounds kosher salt
2 tablespoons vegetable oil, if using aluminum foil

Preheat the oven to 400° F. Rinse and dry the fish thoroughly. Whisk together the egg whites and ½ cup cold water and combine it with the salt in a large mixing bowl. Work the mixture with your hands to distribute the water and egg whites in the salt. The salt mixture should hold together when you press a mound of it together between the palms of your hands. If it doesn't, work in another egg white.

If you're using a baking dish, select an oval one about 2 inches longer than the salmon. Fill the baking dish about a third full with the salt mixture and place the salmon on top. Cover the top and sides of the fish with the rest of the salt mixture and smooth over the salt with your hands or a spatula.

If you're using aluminum foil, roll out a sheet of aluminum foil 3½ times the length of the salmon. Fold the aluminum foil over itself lengthwise until you have a 10-inch wide triple-thick strip that's still 3½ times the length of the salmon. Brush a sheet pan with oil and place the salmon on top. Place the aluminum foil around the fish and shape the foil so that it curves all around the fish with about 1 inch between fish and foil. Attach the ends of the aluminum foil strip with a paper clip or by just pinching the top of one end over the other end. Lift the salmon off the sheet pan and fill the mold with about ⅓ of the salt mixture—there should be a ½-to ¾-inch thick layer of salt. Place the salmon on top. Spread the rest of the salt mixture over and around the fish and smooth over its surface with your hands.

Bake the salmon for 40 minutes to an hour. Start checking the temperature after 40 minutes by inserting an instant-read thermometer through the layer of salt. (You may have to twist and push a little to get the thermometer to penetrate through the salt.) When the fish measures 125° F, take it out of the oven and let it sit for 15 minutes so the heat will continue to penetrate to the middle.

Bring the fish to the table on its sheet pan or on a large platter—something big enough to catch flying salt—and crack the salt crust with a mallet or a hammer. Pull back the salt layer and peel off the skin with a fork. Serve on hot plates in the same way as whole poached salmon (see page 109).

ROAST WHOLE OR CENTER-CUT SALMON

When you buy a salmon to roast, make sure it's not too long to fit diagonally into your largest sheet pan. If you get it home and find that it is, you can cut off the head and trim the tail (some of the drama will be lost) or even cut it in half (all the drama will be lost). I like to serve this salmon with the Tarragon Sauce on page 115 or the Morel Emulsion on page 39.

MAKES 4 TO 10 MAIN-COURSE SERVINGS, DEPENDING
ON THE SIZE OF THE SALMON

> **one 3- to 5-pound center-cut salmon "roast"** or
> **one 4- to 7-pound whole salmon,** scaled
> **salt**
> **pepper**
> **2 tablespoons olive oil**

Preheat the oven to 400° F. Season the salmon on all sides with salt and pepper and rub it with olive oil. Cover a large sheet pan with aluminum foil and rub the foil with olive oil. Place the salmon on the sheet pan and slide it into the oven.

Check the salmon after 20 minutes. If it starts to spatter and smoke or the skin forms large brown blisters, turn the heat down to 350° F and check again in 10 minutes. If the skin hasn't browned enough, turn the heat to 425° F (or even 450° F). A 4-pound whole salmon will cook in 20 to 30 minutes, while a large salmon or a thick 4-pound center-cut section may take as long as 50 minutes. Forty-five minutes is typical for an average large salmon or center-cut section. Check the doneness of the salmon by sticking an instant-read thermometer in the back toward the backbone. Remove the salmon from the oven when the temperature reaches 130° F. Let it rest in a warm place, covered loosely with aluminum foil (covered tightly it will steam and the skin will loose its crispiness), for 15 to 20 minutes, by which time the internal temperature should reach 135° F.

Serve the salmon in the same ways as the poached salmon on page 109, but leave the skin on.

COLD SALMON AND TOMATO
TERRINE WITH OLIVE CREAM

When I began apprenticing in restaurants, seafood terrines were all the rage and they were pretty much all the same. The fish was pureed and an enormous amount of heavy cream was worked into it before the terrine was gently baked. I always found the effect monotonous and the terrines overly rich. But the idea of seafood terrines has always interested me. On a recent trip to the south of France, I encountered a terrine made with fresh sardines and tomatoes, so when I got home I decided to make it with salmon. The olive cream is similar to the Provençal olive and caper spread *tapenade*, except the olive cream is smoother and more saucelike. You can bake the tomatoes the day before you make the terrine. You will need a 6-cup terrine or loaf pan.

MAKES 8 FIRST-COURSE SERVINGS

6 pounds ripe red tomatoes

⅓ cup + 4 tablespoons extra virgin olive oil

3 cloves garlic, crushed, and peeled

one 1¾-pound salmon fillet with the skin on and the pin bones removed

salt

pepper

1½ packets unflavored gelatin, softened in ¼ cup cold water
  in a heat-proof mixing bowl

4 to 6 slices cold-smoked salmon (optional)

For the olive cream:

1 cup brine-cured black olives (not canned), pitted

½ cup heavy cream

Preheat the oven to 400° F. Peel the tomatoes by plunging them in boiling water for 30 seconds, rinsing them immediately with cold water, and pulling away the peels. Cut out the stem end, cut the tomatoes in half crosswise and squeeze out the seeds. Rub a roasting pan or sheet pan with sides with 2 tablespoons of extra-virgin olive oil and place the tomatoes, flat-side down, in the pan. Put the garlic cloves in the pan and drizzle over ⅓ cup of the extra-virgin olive oil.

Bake until the tomatoes are soft, all the liquid released by the tomatoes has completely evaporated, and only olive oil remains in the pan, 2 to 3 hours. Keep a close eye so you don't burn the tomatoes. If the roasting pan caramelizes and threatens to burn in the corners before the liquid has all evaporated, take it out of the oven (leave the oven on for cooking the salmon) and place it on the stove over high heat.

Gently push the tomatoes around with a wooden spoon to evaporate the liquid. Transfer the tomatoes to a stainless steel bowl and deglaze the roasting pan with a cup of water. Boil the water and scrape the bottom of the roasting pan with a wooden spoon to dissolve any caramelized juices. Pour the hot liquid into a measuring cup. You should have ⅔ cups. If you have less, thin it with hot water. If you have more, boil it down to ⅔ cups. Add the hot liquid to the bowl with the softened gelatin. Stir the mixture until the gelatin dissolves and then stir it into the still-warm tomatoes. Season the tomato mixture to taste with salt and pepper, keeping in mind that it will taste less salty when it's cold.

While the tomatoes are roasting, slice the salmon into ½-inch thick escalopes. Cut the escalopes so they have the same width as the mold or loaf pan, but the exact length of the escalopes isn't terribly important. You should have enough escalopes to make 3 layers in the mold. Season the escalopes with salt and pepper and rub them with a tablespoon of the olive oil. Refrigerate, covered with plastic wrap, until needed.

Rub a sheet pan with the last tablespoon of olive oil and arrange the salmon escalopes on the sheet pan in a single layer. Bake the salmon for 2 to 4 minutes in a 400° F oven, until the surface of the salmon starts to lose its translucence. Leave the salmon slightly undercooked. Let cool and refrigerate for 30 minutes to 1 hour.

If the tomatoes have cooled off and they're starting to set, place the bowl over medium heat and stir the tomatoes until they feel just a little warm—if they're too hot they'll cook the salmon; if they're too cold the gelatin won't liquify.

The salmon escalopes, ready for assembly.

Layering the salmon escapoles and tomatoes in the terrine.

If you're using a metal loaf pan, line the bottom of it with microwaveable plastic wrap. If you're using a porcelain or enamel terrine, lining isn't necessary. Spread ¼ of the tomato mixture over the bottom of the terrine. Arrange a layer of salmon on top of the tomatoes. Spread a thin sheet of smoked salmon over the cooked salmon and spread another ¼ of the tomato mixture over the salmon. Continue layering in this way until you have 3 layers of salmon and 4 layers of tomatoes.

Finish with a layer of tomatoes. If at any point the tomato mixture seems too loose to support the layers of salmon, refrigerate the terrine to set the layers you've made. If the tomato mixture in the bowl begins to set while you're making the terrine, stir it over a burner for a minute to melt it. When you're finished, cover the terrine with a sheet of plastic wrap and refrigerate for 12 to 24 hours before serving. Unless the terrine has been lined with plastic wrap, run a knife along the sides of the terrine. Place a large plate upside down over the top of the terrine and turn over the whole assembly, keeping the terrine flush against the plate. Lift away the terrine.

Prepare the olive cream by pureeing the olives with ½ cup of water in a blender until smooth, about 30 seconds. Transfer to a bowl, rinse out the blender with the heavy cream, and stir the cream into the olive sauce.

Slice the terrine with a serrated knife. Place a slice of terrine on each of 8 chilled plates and spoon a swirl of the olive cream around and over each slice.

The terrine in the mold.

The terrine after unmolding.

BROILING

I've never been fond of broiling for several reasons. I find broilers, especially home broilers, hard to control and rarely hot enough to produce a crisp brown crust. Since most home broilers are below the oven, I find myself lying on the floor with the broiler door open trying to monitor cooking and browning. When broiling salmon, the broiler pan needs to be covered with aluminum foil—to prevent sticking and making an awful mess—and the fish fat spatters against the broiler heat source, making smoke and smelling up the kitchen. Given a choice, I'd rather sauté or grill.

But there are two ways of broiling salmon that work especially well. One is to broil a large skin-on salmon fillet, skin side up so the skin turns crisp and then finish the salmon in the oven. The other is a fabulous trick I learned in France—broiling thinly sliced salmon directly on a heat-proof plate for just a few seconds, and then brushing the salmon with a flavorful sauce. The sauce can be virtually anything you like, but I find that vinaigrette and mayonnaise sauces work the best. In France we used a light mayonnaise flavored with truffle juice and hazelnut oil.

BROILED SALMON FILLET WITH CRISPY SKIN

The idea behind this dish is to get the salmon skin crisp at nearly the same time the salmon cooks through. This means keeping a close eye on the salmon and moving it closer or farther from the flame. Too close to the flame, the skin will burn; too far and the skin will never brown and turn crisp.

MAKES 4 MAIN-COURSE SERVINGS

four 6- to 8-ounce center cut salmon fillets with the skin on, about
  1-inch thick
½ **recipe brine** (see page 93)
1 tablespoon softened butter
pepper

Soak the salmon in the brine in the refrigerator for 2 hours. Pat dry.

Preheat the broiler. If your broiler isn't part of the oven, also preheat the oven to 400° F. Cover a sheet pan—one you can fit under the broiler—with a sheet of aluminum foil, shiny side up. Calculate where on the sheet pan you're going to place the salmon and rub that part of the foil with a teaspoon of butter. Place the salmon, flesh side down, on the sheet pan. Slide the salmon under the broiler—start with the top of the salmon about 6 inches away from the heat source—and broil, moving the sheet pan as needed so all the salmon gets the same amount of heat. If the skin starts to bubble up or burn within 4 minutes, move the sheet pan so it's farther from the heat source. If after 3 minutes the skin shows no sign of browning, move the sheet pan closer to the heat source.

When the skin is brown and crisp, ideally after about 6 minutes, move the sheet pan to the oven, or turn the oven you used for broiling to bake and the temperature down to 400° F. Bake the salmon until it is done, about 3 minutes more for a 1-inch thick fillet. Sprinkle the fillet with pepper, brush it with the remaining butter, and serve it in slices on hot plates.

QUICK-BROILED SALMON WITH MUSTARD AND HAZELNUT OIL

The time-consuming part of this dish—slicing the salmon—can be done earlier the day you plan to serve it.

MAKES 4 MAIN-COURSE SERVINGS

- 1½ **pounds salmon fillet with the skin on and pin bones removed that has been frozen** (see page 117), from the tail end, in one piece
- 1 **tablespoon Dijon mustard**
- ½ **teaspoon salt,** preferably sea salt
- 1 **teaspoon wine vinegar**
- 3 **tablespoons roasted hazelnut oil or extra-virgin olive oil**

Place a sheet of waxed paper on top of one of the heat-proof plates.

Slice the salmon into thin slices as you would raw salmon carpaccio (see recipe on page 118) and arrange the slices on the waxed paper with the least attractive side facing up. Follow the shape of the plate, keeping in mind that the waxed paper is going to be turned down onto the plate at the last minute. Continue in this way until you have 4 sheets of waxed paper covered with raw salmon slices. If you've sliced the salmon ahead of time, spread the sheets of salmon on a sheet pan—you can overlap them but don't stack them—cover the sheet pan with plastic wrap, and refrigerate until needed.

Shortly before serving, heat the plates in a 200° F oven.

Combine the mustard, salt, and vinegar in a small mixing bowl and whisk in the hazelnut oil. The sauce should taste quite salty and strong since it's the only seasoning that the salmon will get.

Immediately before serving, turn on the broiler—unless you have two ovens this will mean taking out the plates—and turn one of the salmon-covered sheets of waxed paper down on one of the plates, centering the salmon on the plate. Peel back the waxed paper. Don't lift it away from the plate or the salmon will stick to the paper, but pull it to one side so it peels away. Hold the plate under the broiler with an oven mitt from about 20 seconds to a minute, rotating the plate so the salmon cooks evenly until it just loses its sheen. Repeat immediately with the other 3 plates. Brush or spoon a thin layer of the sauce (it's very salty) over the salmon and serve immediately.

Salmon in almost any form makes delicious traditional sandwiches as well as the open-faced sandwiches on crusty bread that the Italians call bruschette. Sandwiches and bruschette are a great way to serve salmon left over from the night before.

MAKES 4 GENEROUS SANDWICHES

8 slices crusty French bread

butter or extra-virgin olive oil

4 broiled, sautéed, or grilled salmon fillets, ¼- to ½-inch thick

salt

pepper

4 thin slices cold-smoked salmon (optional)

8 thin slices red onion (optional)

8 thin slice ripe tomato (optional)

4 pieces lettuce, preferably a crunchy variety such as romaine

1 ripe avocado, preferably Hass, peeled, pitted, and sliced

½ lime

Toast the slices of bread. Butter 4 of the slices or brush them with olive oil on one side. If you didn't season the salmon when you cooked it, sprinkle it with salt and pepper. Stack the salmon, smoked salmon, onion, tomato, and lettuce on the 4 slices of buttered toast. Spread the avocado slices evenly over the other ingredients, squeeze a little lime juice over it, and season with salt and pepper. Cover with the remaining bread slices.

SALMON "NAPOLEONS"

These elegant little first courses require a light touch and a bit of fiddling in the kitchen. I serve them when I'm feeling extravagant or when giving a dinner party for very dear friends or people I want to impress. A napoleon, of course, is a sweet pastry made by layering sheets of cooked puff pastry with pastry cream, cutting the sheets into rectangles, and glazing the top with fondant, a kind of sugar glaze. The idea of a savory napoleon is not new—I've encountered several versions in fancy restaurants—but there's still plenty of room for invention.

I make salmon napoleons with thin layers of salmon that have been broiled for just a few seconds. I then layer these rectangles with tiny cubes of cucumber and smoked salmon and top the whole thing off with real black caviar or less expensive salmon roe. Cooking the salmon and preparing the cucumber mixture can be done earlier the day you plan to serve them, but the napoleons should be constructed just before serving or the roe or caviar will dry out.

MAKES 6 FIRST-COURSE SERVINGS

> 1 long hot-house cucumber or 2 regular cucumbers, peeled
> 1 tablespoon coarse salt
> one 1-pound piece of salmon fillet
> pepper
> 1 tablespoon softened butter
> 2 tablespoons crème fraîche
> 3 thin slices cold smoked salmon
> 3 ounces osetra, sevruga, or beluga caviar, or salmon roe

Cut the cucumber in half lengthwise and scoop the seeds out of each half with a spoon. Slice the cucumber lengthwise into strips between ⅛- and ¼-inch thick. Slice the strips crosswise so you end up with ⅛- to ¼-inch cubes. (This is easier if you use a plastic slicer—the Benriner brand is my favorite—to slice the cucumbers before you cut them into strips and then dice. Remember that the cubes will shrink after they've been salted.) Toss the cubes with the coarse salt, rubbing the cubes with the salt for a minute or two until you can't feel the crystals under your fingers. Put the cubes in a strainer over a bowl and set in the refrigerator to drain for an hour or until you're ready to construct the napoleons, up to 8 hours.

Using a long, thin knife, slice the salmon into twelve ¼-inch thick rectangles about 3 inches long and 1½ inches wide. Trim the slices so they're the same size (you can freeze the trimmings and use them for the salmon tartare on page 117). Season the salmon slices on both sides with pepper (no salt is used because the cucumbers and caviar are already salty). Cover a sheet pan with a sheet of aluminum foil—shiny side up—and rub it with butter. Arrange the salmon rectangles, near each other but not touching, on the foil. Preheat the broiler and hold the sheet pan under the broiler, moving it around so the pieces of salmon are exposed to the same amount of heat, until the salmon rectangles no longer appear raw on top. This usually takes from 30 seconds to 1 minute. Whatever you do, don't overcook the salmon, which will make it fragile and very difficult to work with. Let the salmon cool at room temperature and then refrigerate it for 15 minutes to 4 hours.

Squeeze the cucumber cubes tightly in a clean kitchen towel—rinse out the towel first to eliminate any traces of soap—to get rid of as much liquid as possible. You should end up with about 1 cup of cubes. Combine the cubes in a small bowl with the crème fraîche.

Cut the smoked salmon slices into rectangles the same size as the fresh salmon. You can patch together pieces of the smoked salmon in the napoleons—no one will see it.

Spread about 1 tablespoon of the cucumber mixture evenly over 6 slices of the salmon and place a layer of smoked salmon on top. Spread another layer of the cucumber mixture over the smoked salmon and gently place a rectangle of cooked salmon on top. You can prepare the napoleons up to this stage several hours before serving and keep them covered with plastic wrap in the refrigerator.

Gently spread a layer of caviar or salmon roe on top of each napoleon. Gently press around the sides of the napoleons to push in any cucumber that's trying to ooze out. Serve immediately.

What If Your Fillets Are of Uneven Thickness? Even center-cut salmon fillets often have a section of belly flap that is thinner than the rest of the fillet, making it impossible to cook the fillet evenly. When I'm broiling skin-off fillets, I cut the skin off the end of the belly flap and fold the flap under the rest of the fillet so the fillet rests evenly, and all the same thickness, on the baking sheet.

OTHER WAYS
TO COOK
SALMON

You can cook salmon using virtually any method you would for cooking other seafood or even meat. In this chapter I've adapted some of my favorite dishes—a Moroccan-style chicken stew called a tagine, ravioli, and little-open faced sandwiches (bruschette)—to include salmon.

There are very few basic techniques for cooking salmon—baking, roasting, grilling to name some—but you can come up with myriad variations by combining techniques (such as baking the salmon for the terrine on page 133) or by accompanying a single piece of cooked salmon with a particular sauce. In this book, I've offered a number of sauces that can be dolloped on a piece of grilled, sautéed, or poached salmon, but you can also invent your own salmon dishes by substituting salmon in seafood soups or in various stews, seafood or otherwise.

Regardless of how you cook your salmon, keep one thing in mind. Unlike meats, which are cooked to various temperatures depending on the type and cut, salmon should never be cooked to an internal temperature higher than 137° F or it will dry out. For this reason, you may have to cook the other ingredients called for in a soup or stew and only add the salmon shortly before serving. Because salmon, once cooked, is also fragile, you can't use it in dishes such as stir-frying that require rough treatment or it will fall apart.

SAUTÉED SALMON IN THE STYLE OF
A TAGINE WITH COUSCOUS

Various styles of tagines are found throughout North Africa, but my favorites are from Morocco. Moroccan cooks make many different fish tagines but never use salmon, which isn't found anywhere near Morocco. This version isn't authentic— in fact, it's more akin to a chicken tagine—but the juxtaposition of spices, dried fruits, and almonds is entirely Moroccan, so this delicious dish is at least authentic in spirit. The sauce can be made up to 3 days ahead and refrigerated or up to several months ahead and frozen.

MAKES 6 MAIN-COURSE SERVINGS

> **six 6- to 8-ounce pieces salmon fillet with skin on or off and pin bones removed**
> **salt**
> **pepper**
> **6 tablespoons slivered almonds**
> **1 medium onion,** chopped fine
> **2 cloves garlic,** chopped fine
> **2 tablespoons olive oil**
> **1 teaspoon ground turmeric or 2 teaspoons finely chopped fresh**
> **2 tablespoons finely grated fresh ginger**
> **1 teaspoon ground cinnamon**
> **¼ teaspoon ground cloves**
> **2 cups chicken broth**
> **½ cup dried apricots, cut into ¼-inch dice**
> **½ cup golden raisins**
> **1 teaspoon saffron threads or ¼ teaspoon powdered saffron**
> **harissa** (see page 147)
> **plain couscous,** for serving

Season the salmon with salt and pepper and refrigerate until needed. Toast the almonds in a 350° F oven for 15 minutes or in a heavy-bottomed pan over a low heat for 10 minutes, until they turn pale brown and smell fragrant.

Stir the onion and garlic with a tablespoon of the olive oil in a heavy-bottomed saucepan. Cook over medium heat, stirring every couple of minutes, until the onions turn translucent but aren't brown, about 10 minutes. Stir in the turmeric, ginger, cinnamon, and cloves and cook over medium heat for 1 minute more— until you smell the fragrance of the spices. Add the broth, bring to a simmer, and simmer gently for 5 minutes. Put the mixture in a blender and puree—be careful and start out with short pulses, holding the lid firmly with your hand wrapped in a towel—for about 30 seconds. Work the mixture through a strainer set over the rinsed-out pan. Bring back to a simmer and add the apricots, raisins, and saffron. Simmer for 5 minutes and season to taste with salt and pepper.

Prepare the couscous according to the directions on the package.

Sauté, bake, or grill the salmon and place each piece in the center of heated plates, ideally soup plates. Spoon the sauce around the salmon, sprinkle the almonds over it, swirl in a spoonful of harissa. Pass the rest of the harissa at the table. Serve the couscous at the table or put a mound on each plate.

Every Mediterranean country seems to have its garlicky condiment to dollop on various seafood and meat stews. The French have their aïoli and rouille, the Spanish have picada and romesco, and the Italians have pesto. But one of the most complex and delicious of all these concoctions is the Moroccan harissa, a mixture of caraway, coriander, curry, chilies, garlic, and olive oil. A spoonful of harissa is delicious on just about anything.

MAKES 1 CUP

- **6 dried ancho or guajillo chilies,** dust wiped off with a damp towel
- **1 tablespoon whole caraway seeds**
- **1 tablespoon whole coriander seeds**
- **1 teaspoon curry powder**
- **2 cloves garlic,** chopped fine, and crushed to a paste with the side of a chefs' knife
- **1 teaspoon salt,** or more as needed
- **1 ripe tomato,** peeled, halved crosswise, seeds squeezed out, and chopped
- **⅓ cup extra-virgin olive oil**

Cut the stem ends off the chilies, cut them in half lengthwise, and brush out their seeds. Place them in a dry skillet or heavy-bottomed sauté pan over high heat, turning them around every minute, until they smell fragrant, 3 to 5 minutes. Chop them coarsely and place them, with the caraway, coriander, and curry powder, in a blender. Blend the ingredients at high speed for about 1 minute until you end up with a coarse powder. Add the garlic, salt, and tomato to the blender and blend for 1 minute more. Transfer the mixture to a mixing bowl and work in the olive oil, a few teaspoons at a time with a wooden spoon. Don't use a whisk. (For some mysterious reason, extra-virgin olive oil turns bitter when beaten.) Add more salt if needed. Stir the harissa just before serving, because it tends to separate as it sits.

TOMATO, BASIL, AND SALMON BRUSCHETTE

You can make these open-faced Italian sandwiches any size you like. I like to make them small—using baguette slices—and give 3 per serving as a snack or 1 or 2 per serving as an hors d'oeuvre. You can use cold salmon in virtually any form—grilled, sautéed, hot-smoked, or cold- smoked—or you can spread the toasts with the rillettes on page 101. These bruschette are topped with chopped basil and chopped tomatoes, but you can use anything you like as a topping, including any of the sauces suggested for grilled salmon (see page 63). The chili mayonnaise is especially good.

MAKES 4 SNACK SERVINGS OR 12 HORS-D'OEUVRE SERVINGS

> **4 ripe medium tomatoes**
> **salt**
> **pepper**
> **12 slices French bread, about ¼-inch thick,** toasted on both sides
> **1 garlic clove,** peeled (optional)
> **4 tablespoons extra-virgin olive oil**
> **leaves from one bunch of basil, about 30**
> **12 slices grilled, sautéed, hot-smoked, or cold-smoked salmon,**
>   **or 1 recipe salmon rillettes** (see page 101) **chilled**

Using a slotted spoon, submerge the tomatoes, 2 at a time, into about 2 quarts of boiling water for about 30 seconds and immediately rinse them with cold water. Cut out the stem end with a paring knife and pull the peels away. Cut the tomatoes in half crosswise and squeeze out and discard their seeds. Chop coarsely and season to taste with salt and pepper. Unless you're using them right away, keep the tomatoes in a strainer over a bowl so any liquid they release drains off.

Rub each slice of toast with the garlic clove and brush or spoon about a teaspoon of olive oil over each slice.

Rub the basil leaves with about 2 teaspoons of olive oil—to keep them from turning dark—and chop them coarse. Spread the chopped basil on top of each toast.

Arrange the salmon on top of each toast and season it with salt and pepper unless it's smoked or you've already seasoned it when you cooked it. Just before serving, spoon a mound of the tomatoes over the salmon.

Salmon with Pasta

Fettuccine with smoked salmon seemed to be on every menu the last time I was in Italy and, while it's perfectly good (just simmer a little chopped smoked salmon in some heavy cream and toss with the cooked pasta), I always search out more traditional fare, figuring I can make the other stuff at home. Having never come across salmon ravioli—odd, because the idea sounded lovely—I decided to make my own. There are several ways to make your own ravioli, which are all easier than they sound, but there are a couple of pitfalls to watch out for. First, if the filling doesn't contain some fat that will melt and burst in your mouth when the ravioli is hot, the filling will taste flat and dry. Second, many cooks surround ravioli or other stuffed pasta with a sauce that tastes similar to the filling, which makes biting into the ravioli itself a bit of an anticlimax. I like to serve ravioli surrounded by a light broth—what the Italians call *in brodo*—so the effect of the salmon is all the more dramatic. When I'm feeling like something a bit more extravagant, I make a simple cream sauce by simmering heavy cream with a little fresh tarragon. Salmon ravioli are also a great way to use leftover salmon, spinach, or Swiss chard.

Making ravioli with wonton wrappers.

SALMON AND BASIL RAVIOLI

This recipe can be changed by substituting different herbs, or using fresh bread crumbs and olive oil instead of butter, but regardless of how you modify the recipe, remember that the salmon should be chopped fine, but not to the consistency of a puree or it will feel pasty and dry in your mouth. The filling for these ravioli can be made with raw salmon or salmon cooked earlier in the day you plan to serve them, or several weeks ahead of time and frozen. You can also make the uncooked ravioli ahead of time and freeze them on a sheet pan—spaced so they don't touch—and storing the frozen ravioli in plastic bags. Don't try to freeze them directly in plastic bags or they'll stick together.

MAKES 48 RAVIOLI
8 FIRST-COURSE SERVINGS OR 4 MAIN-COURSE SERVINGS

- **1 pound raw** (previously frozen, see page 117), **hot-smoked, or grilled salmon**
- **½ pound cold unsalted butter**
- **leaves from 1 large bunch basil, about 60,** washed and dried
- **2 tablespoons olive oil**
- **2 small cloves garlic,** chopped fine, and crushed to a paste with the side of a chefs' knife
- **2 shallots,** chopped fine
- **1 tablespoon salt** (less if you're using hot-smoked or grilled salmon that has been brined or seasoned—if the filling is made with cooked salmon, just salt to taste; if it's made with raw salmon, make a sample ravioli before tasting)
- **1 teaspoon freshly ground black pepper**
- **1 recipe fresh pasta** (see page 152) **or 48 thin round wonton wrappers** (about 1 package)
- **4 cups flavorful chicken broth**
- **1 tablespoon fresh marjoram leaves,** chopped at the last minute, **or 8 fresh whole sage leaves** (optional)

Cut the salmon and butter into ¼ inch cubes and chop the mixture to the consistency of hamburger by hand or in a food processor. If you're using a food processor, the filling is ready the instant it starts to form a ball.

Rub the basil leaves with 1 tablespoon of the olive oil—and chop fine. Stir the basil, garlic, shallots, salt, and pepper into the salmon mixture with a heavy wooden spoon. If you're not using the filling right away, cover it with plastic wrap and refrigerate it until needed, but not for longer than 24 hours.

If you're using the pasta, roll it out and stuff the ravioli using about a tablespoon of filling per ravioli as described on the next page. If you're using wonton wrappers, stuff them as also described on the next page.

Bring about 6 cups of water to a boil with the remaining olive oil. Bring the chicken broth to a simmer with the chopped marjoram or whole sage leaves.

Put the ravioli in the water all at once. When the water comes back to a simmer, turn down the heat. Cooking the ravioli at a rapid boil could cause them to burst open.

When the ravioli are done—you'll need to bite into one to know when they're ready but they usually take 6 minutes when made with pasta and 4 minutes when made with wonton wrappers—drain them in a colander and distribute them among heated soup plates. Season the broth to taste with salt and pepper and ladle it over the ravioli. If you've used sage leaves, put 2 in every first course serving and 1 in every main course serving.

Pasta Dough: Combine 3 cups flour, 4 large eggs, and a tablespoon of olive oil in a food processor and pulse the mixture about 20 times, until it has the texture of coarse sand. Pour it out onto the work surface and knead it with the heel of your hand until it forms a ball. You may need to sprinkle it with water if it won't come together, or knead it with a little flour if it feels sticky.

To roll out the dough with a pasta machine, roll about ⅓ of the dough through the machine at its widest setting. Fold the dough over itself 2 or 3 times and roll it again through the machine until it is smooth and elastic and feels a bit like suede. Start rolling the dough through the machine, setting the thickness to a thinner setting after each roll until you end up with thin sheets. If you're not using the pasta right away, you can keep it on a sheet pan, tightly covered with plastic wrap, for a couple of hours.

Making Ravioli: There are 4 ways to make ravioli, 3 of which require making your own pasta. Once you've rolled out thin sheets of pasta— by hand or with a pasta machine—you can cut out squares or rounds with a pasta cutter and then spoon or pipe (with a pastry bag) a dollop of filling in the center, moisten the outer rim of the square or round, and set a second square or round on top, pinching it around on all sides to seal in the filling. You can also use the ravioli-maker attachment to your pasta machine or use a hand ravioli maker, which is a rectangular metal plate with a dozen rounds cut out of it. You roll the pasta dough over the plate, and push the pasta down with a piece of plastic that looks vaguely like an egg holder, which creates a place for the filling. You then brush around the edges with water—to help seal them—and spoon or pipe in the filling before rolling another sheet of pasta over them. You then roll over the top of the whole contraption with a rolling pin, and you end up with a dozen ravioli. The last method, and the easiest since you don't need to make pasta, is to place a dollop of filling just to the right of the center of thin round wonton wrappers that have been brushed with water, fold over the left side of the wrapper, and seal in the filling by pinching around the edges with your fingers.

If you're making your own pasta dough, roll it out into 18-inch long sheets and place a tablespoon of the filling in small mounds (1 tablespoon per mound) along two rows running the length of the pasta. Leave enough space between each mound to seal in the filling. Brush the pasta with cold water between the filling mounds and along the edges of the dough. Roll out a second sheet of dough and unroll it over the first. Press between the mounds with your fingers, sealing the filling in the dough. Cut the dough into squares with a knife or fluted pastry cutter or with a square or round pasta cutter. Pinch the edges of each ravioli to make sure the filling is well sealed within. Until you're ready to cook them, reserve the ravioli on a sheet pan covered liberally with semolina flour, corn meal, or olive oil to prevent the ravioli from sticking to the pan.

Using the Microwave

Many of us shun the microwave as somehow being unwholesome, its invisible heat somehow suspect. I've never shared a blind aversion to the microwave—it's great for heating up soups, plates, and certain leftovers—but I am aware of its pitfalls and idiosyncrasies. First, it heats foods unevenly. Newer microwaves with rotating platforms help this problem somewhat but not completely. (Someone has yet to invent a platform that both rotates and moves up and down for even heating.) Second, the microwave's efficiency depends on how much food you put in it at one time. In a regular oven it takes no longer to cook 16 baked potatoes than it does one, but in the average microwave cooking a large amount of anything starts to take longer than the oven. This being said, the microwave is best for cooking small amounts of food—one or two servings—and something must be done to get foods to cook through evenly. My own trick for salmon consists of cooking it in a covered container with a small amount of liquid, so it steams at the same time it's being heated through by the microwaves. I turn the microwave off after a minute, allowing the heat to distribute itself more evenly throughout the salmon. I then cook it a minute more—still covered—and wait another minute after that.

MICROWAVED SALMON WITH WHITE WINE BUTTER SAUCE

If you want to make just one serving, use half the amount of each ingredient listed below and cook the salmon in the microwave for 2 minutes, let it rest for 1 minute, then cook again for 1 minute, and let it rest for 1 minute more.

If you cook the salmon in decorative containers—I use oval porcelain gratin dishes—you can serve it in the same dishes you cooked the salmon in. Otherwise, I transfer the salmon to soup plates—to hold the runny sauce—pour the sauce over and around, and serve with spoons to slurp up the sauce.

MAKES 2 MAIN-COURSE SERVINGS

- **two 6-to 8-ounce salmon steaks or fillets**
- **salt**
- **pepper**
- **3 tablespoons dry white wine**
  - **or dry sherry** (such as fino)
- **1 tablespoon fine chopped parsley**
- **2 tablespoons unsalted butter**

If you're using salmon steaks, you may want to tie them into medallions as described on page 20, but this is less important than when poaching or grilling because in the microwave, the belly flaps cook at the same time as the center.

Season the salmon with salt and pepper and place the steaks or fillets in a container just large enough to hold them in a single layer. Pour the wine and 2 tablespoons of water over them, sprinkle the parsley on top, and place 1 table-spoon of butter on each piece of salmon. Cover the container with microwavable plastic wrap—poke a hole in it with a pin, which allows steam to escape but is small enough so the heat is held in—or a microwaveable lid.

Microwave the salmon on high for 2 minutes, let rest 1 minute—don't lift off the plastic wrap—heat for 2 minutes more and let rest for 2 minutes more, for a total cooking time of 7 minutes. Cooking times may vary slightly depending on the microwave.

Use a spatula to transfer the salmon to heated soup plates. Provided they don't have any metal on them, I heat the plates in the microwave right under the salmon. Spoon the juices in the dish over the salmon and serve.

Variation: Because for most of us, the purpose of using the microwave is speed and convenience, I've kept the basic microwave recipe as simple as possible, but you can vary it by adding other liquids instead of the wine and water (finely chopped tomatoes, or the cooking liquid from mushrooms or shellfish such as mussels are a some possibilities). When the salmon is done, I sometimes pour the liquid into a saucepan, boil it down slightly, and add 2 or 3 tablespoons of heavy cream to give it a more saucelike consistency. You can also replace or augment the parsley with other herbs, such as chives, tarragon, or chervil.

SOURCES

Dried Chilies

The CMC Company
P. O. Drawer B
Avalon, NJ 08202
800-262-2780
www.thecmccompany.com

Dean and Deluca
560 Broadway
New York, NY 10012
www.deandeluca.com

www.ethnicgrocer.com
Customer Service:
800-523-1961

www.querico.com
800-523-1963

Japanese Ingredients

Katagiri
224 East 59th Street
New York, NY 10022
212-755-3566
www.katagiri.com

The CMC Company
P. O. Drawer B
Avalon, NJ 08202
800-262-2780
www.thecmccompany.com

Dean and Deluca
560 Broadway
New York, NY 10012
www.deandeluca.com

www.ethnicgrocer.com
Customer Service:
800-523-1961

Kitchen Equipment

J. B. Prince
800-473-0577 or
212-683-3553
www.jbprince.com

Broadway Panhandler
477 Broome Street
New York, NY 10013
212-966-3434
www.broadwaypanhandler.com

Sur la Table
800-243-0852
www.surlatable.com

Williams-Sonoma
800-699-2297
www.williams-sonoma.com

Roasted Nut Oils

Rosenthal Wine Merchants,
Ltd.   518-398-1800
www.madrose.com/home2.
html

Thai, Vietnamese. and other Asian Ingredients

The Oriental Pantry
423 Great Road
Acton, MA 01720
800-828-0368
www.orientalpantry.com

The CMC Company
P. O. Drawer B
Avalon, NJ 08202
800-262-2780
www.thecmccompany.com

Penzey's Spices
P.O. Box 933
Muskego, WI 53150
www.penzeys.com

www.ethnicgrocer.com
Customer Service:
800-523-1961

Spice Merchant
P.O. Box 524
Jackson Hole, WY 83001
307-733-7811
www.email.com/spice/

Hard-Wood and Fruit-Wood Sawdust and Chips

The Sausage Maker
   (sawdust only)
888-490-8525
FAX: 716-824-6465

Broadway Panhandler
477 Broome Street
New York, NY 10013
212-966-3434
www.broadwaypanhandler.
com

Oven-style Hot Smoker

The Sausage Maker
888-490-8525
FAX: 716-824-6465

Wild Mushrooms

Marché aux Delices
(dried and fresh)
888-547-5471
www.auxdelices.com

Rosenthal Wine Merchants,
Ltd.
   (dried only)
518-398-1800
www.madrose.com/home2.
html

Urbani USA
(fresh, dried, and frozen)
800-281-2330
www.urbani.com

In Canada

The Gourmet Warehouse
1856 Pandora Street
Lane entrance
Vancouver, BC
604-253-3022
www.gourmetwarehouse-
canada.com
V5L 1M5

Pusateri's
1539 Avenue Road
Toronto, ON
M5M 3X4
416-785-9100
www.pusateris.com

CONVERSION CHART

Weight Equivalents

The metric weights given in this chart are not exact equivalents, but have been rounded up or down slightly to make measuring easier.

AVOIRDUPOIS	METRIC
¼ oz	7 g
½ oz	15 g
1 oz	30 g
2 oz	60 g
3 oz	90 g
4 oz	115 g
5 oz	150 g
6 oz	175 g
7 oz	200 g
8 oz (½ lb)	225 g
9 oz	250 g
10 oz	300 g
11 oz	325 g
12 oz	350 g
13 oz	375 g
14 oz	400 g
15 oz	425 g
16 oz (1 lb)	450 g
1½ lb	750 g
2 lb	900 g
2¼ lb	1 kg
3 lb	1.4 kg
4 lb	1.8 kg

Volume Equivalents

These are not exact equivalents for American cups and spoons, but have been rounded up or down slightly to make measuring easier.

AMERICAN	METRIC	IMPERIAL
¼ t	1.2 ml	
½ t	2.5 ml	
1 t	5.0 ml	
½ T (1.5 t)	7.5 ml	
1 T (3 t)	15 ml	
¼ cup (4 T)	60 ml	2 fl oz
⅓ cup (5 T)	75 ml	2½ fl oz
½ cup (8 T)	125 ml	4 fl oz
⅔ cup (10 T)	150 ml	5 fl oz
¾ cup (12 T)	175 ml	6 fl oz
1 cup (16 T)	250 ml	8 fl oz
1¼ cups	300 ml	10 fl oz (½ pt)
1½ cups	350 ml	12 fl oz
2 cups (1 pint)	500 ml	16 fl oz
2½ cups	625 ml	20 fl oz (1 pint)
1 quart	1 liter	32 fl oz

Oven Temperature Equivalents

OVEN MARK	F	C	GAS
Very cool	250–275	130–140	½–1
Cool	300	150	2
Warm	325	170	3
Moderate	350	180	4
Moderately hot	375	190	5
	400	200	6
Hot	425	220	7
	450	230	8
Very hot	475	250	9

INDEX

(Page numbers in *italic* refer to illustrations.)

Acknowledgments

I'm amazed by the number of people and how hard they work to turn a manuscript into a book. First, I'd like to thank my editor and publisher, Leslie Stoker, for her enthusiasm for the project and for thinking up the idea in the first place. Thanks to Nina Barnett for the design of the book and to Kim Tyner for supervising the production. And thanks to Jack Lamplough for his help promoting *Simply Salmon.* I would also like to thank Ann ffolliott for her careful copyediting. Thanks must go to Christina Burridge, who reviewed the introductory material and to Terri Wershler who deepened my knowledge of West Coast salmon. I'm also very appreciative of John Bishop's lovely introduction to the Canadian edition.

While photographing the images for *Simply Salmon,* I was privileged to work with three of New York's best food stylists: Ann Disrude, Sally Schneider, and Dora Jonassen. Debre DeMers helped during the photography by assisting but also by offering her sense of design and her wonderful humor. And many thanks to the guys at Fish Tales, my neighborhood fish store, for their great fish.

As always, I thank my agents, Elise and Arnold Goodman, who do far more than negociate contracts; they listen, give gentle advice, and always make themselves available. Finally, thanks to Zelik Mintz, my life-partner and food guinea pig, who was recently served the following menu:

Salmon Carpaccio with Extra Virgin Olive Oil and Balsamic Vinegar
Salmon Tartare
Hot-Smoked Salmon Rillettes
Sautéed Salmon "Saltimbocca"

Fortunately, I've never figured out a salmon dessert.